DOES THIS MEAN YOU'LL SEE ME NAKED?

DOES THIS MEAN YOU'LL ❧ SEE ME NAKED? ❧

A Funeral Director Reflects on 30 Years of
Serving the Living and the Deceased

ROBERT D. WEBSTER

Bloomington, IN Milton Keynes, UK

AuthorHouse™
1663 Liberty Drive, Suite 200
Bloomington, IN 47403
www.authorhouse.com
Phone: 1-800-839-8640

AuthorHouse™ *UK Ltd.*
500 Avebury Boulevard
Central Milton Keynes, MK9 2BE
www.authorhouse.co.uk
Phone: 08001974150

This book is a work of non-fiction. Unless otherwise noted, the author and the publisher make no explicit guarantees as to the accuracy of the information contained in this book and in some cases, names of people and places have been altered to protect their privacy.

First published by AuthorHouse 9/20/2006

ISBN: 1-4259-5658-0 (sc)
ISBN: 1-4259-5659-9 (dj)

Library of Congress Control Number: 2006907229

Printed in the United States of America
Bloomington, Indiana

This book is printed on acid-free paper.

This book is dedicated to my wife, Mel, daughter, Anna, and sons, Michael and Ben for enduring the consequences of my chosen profession. I appreciate the patience afforded me as I was the husband who had to leave the dinner party; the Dad who had to exit early from the school play, and miss many baseball games over the years because someone's family had experienced a death.

Much appreciation to Coleen Armstrong for her push and encouragement to attain this work.

And, a special thank-you to Cindy Blizzard Browning for her comment to me which led to the title of this book.

✂ TABLE OF CONTENTS ✂

ONE   "Mister, I Don't Want My Mom to Be Dead."   1
The many faces of death and those we leave behind

TWO   "Does This Mean You'll See Me Naked?"   7
People's most common fear regarding funerals, body art, final requests and oddest casket inclusions

THREE   "Death by Defecation"   17
Removal of dead bodies, hoisting the morbidly obese and why so many people die while sitting on the toilet

FOUR   "She's Gonna Get Up...She's Gonna Get Up..."   28
Grief, denial and parents who endure the horror of losing their children

FIVE   "I Need to Be Up Front; I Was His Favorite Cousin."   37
The curious custom of sending flowersand why some "mourners" behave so badly

SIX   "Why Would You Want to Hang Out with Dead People?"   48
Why burial is the ultimate solution, how the undertaker's role has evolved, and why we really are full of it

SEVEN   "They Sure Do Good Work Here."   65
Decapitation, restoration, presentation, suicide—and the occasional posthumous bust enlargement •

EIGHT   "Mom's Favorite Grandchild, Freddy..."   79
*Caskets versus coffins, the "leakage" factor, vaults and
mausoleums, cremation, disinterment—and the thorny
business of composing a proper obituary*

NINE   "As Soon As We Sell Dad's House, We'll Pay
          Your Bill."   104
*Who price-shops and who doesn't, who pays on time and
who doesn't, and why today's funeral directors rarely
extend credit*

TEN   "Who's the Hooker with the Minister?"   121
*Whiners, bad apples, altruism, and why dealing with the
clergy can be so high-maintenance*

ELEVEN   "What If You Get Hit by a Bus, and You
          Aren't Prepared?"   139
*The increasing trend toward conglomerates, high-pressure
sales techniques, how the Federal Trade Commission got
involved, and why you may soon see caskets on display at
Wal-Mart*

TWELVE   "And So It Begins..."   152
*Behind the scenes on a death call and what really hap-
pens in the autopsy room*

THIRTEEN   "Would You Really Let Your Daughter
             Drive a Lime Green Hearse?"   162
*A reflection on the success and accuracy of HBO's "Six
Feet Under"*

AFTERWORD   "You Sound Just Like Him."   167
*A funeral director's son speaks out on high standards,
learning patience, being frequently mistaken for "the
man" and how he hopes to continue his father's legacy*

DOES THIS MEAN YOU'LL SEE ME NAKED?

"Mister, I Don't Want My Mom to Be Dead."

*The many faces of death
and those we leave behind*

Arriving at the cemetery, leading a funeral procession through the entrance, I often observe a kindly-looking elderly gentleman seated in a lawn chair facing a black granite headstone. One day, following a short service, I decided to speak to him.

It was, he told me, a monument dedicated to his wife. She had passed away four years earlier, following 44 years of marriage. He could not forget her, nor did he wish to. He would never find anyone else to love and had no intention of trying. So he visited her every day, weather permitting. Even on some of the coldest winter mornings he would show up, sometimes remaining in the warmth of his car's interior, yet still very much present.

He explained to me that he greeted her by name upon arrival, settled into his chair, told her of his daily activities and then said a tender goodbye. Joggers and cemetery personnel steered clear, probably thinking him unbalanced. He didn't care.

To this day, I still wave to him whenever I arrive at the cemetery and again as I depart. His genuine smile of recognition—-and his enduring devotion to his beloved wife—warm my heart.

On the other hand...

A grieving father lay plopped on the ground, his back resting against his late daughter's recently erected monument. I had conducted the funeral for this precious 22-year-old just a few months earlier. At the time of her death, he was an inconsolable basket case—sobbing violently and shaking like some palsy victim.

After the funeral he thanked me, but also admitted that he was thinking of ending his own life so that he might join his daughter in heaven. I informed three separate grief support organizations, and the gentleman was contacted the very next day. One woman who specialized in assisting parents who had lost children reported later that the man seemed to be adjusting well and, in her opinion, was in the healing process of his grief cycle.

But the father had already chosen the day of his daughter's dedication to shoot himself. Cemetery workers noticed him seated at her grave, armed with a handgun, so police were called to the scene. After many tense moments of negotiations and pleading, the father shot himself dead and slumped against the base of his daughter's beautiful pink granite headstone.

And...

An elderly woman approached me at the conclusion of her late husband's funeral and requested that I escort everyone out of the chapel, so that we might be alone. She then asked me to snip a lock of her husband's hair so that she could retain it as a keepsake. I placed it in a plastic bag and handed it to her.

A few weeks later she stopped by to pay off the funeral bill. She reached into her purse and produced a glass baby food jar that contained another lock of hair, this one from her child who had died in 1952. The tightly closed metal lid had kept it in pristine condition for over 50 years.

She also showed me a cracked and faded photograph of that child lying in a casket. She'd made it a habit to gaze upon the aged photo and the lock of hair every morning as a tribute—and she informed me that she now planned the same daily ritual to honor her husband.

And...

When three out of four daughters approached their late father's casket, screams and primal outbursts pierced the scene. The fourth daughter was conspicuously standing off to one side of the chapel by herself, showing very little emotion. The other three sobbed uncontrollably, wailing, "Daddy, oh Daddy!"

The deceased man's wife, the girls' mother, also stood away—another sign that something about this scenario was very odd. When I had removed the deceased from his hospital room days earlier, even the attending nurse seemed strangely indifferent to the death of her patient. "Just get him out of here," she demanded.

I knew the nurse well and later felt comfortable enough to question her. She revealed that the man had confessed to her that he had been sexually abusing his daughters for many years. At first she assumed that pain medication was causing him to hallucinate. But when she mentioned to one daughter that her father was saying some awful things, the woman stopped the nurse in mid-sentence and asked several specific questions.

Finally the daughter affirmed that his story was true. She and two of the four sisters were in fact having sex (and children) with their father. It had begun with rapes when the girls were all under age ten. Over time, however, the girls actually began visiting their father's bedroom and initiating the actions themselves.

Overweight and unattractive, this daughter stated that their father constantly heaped praise upon them, telling them how pretty they were. The mother worked at a nursing home and was the family breadwinner, thus making their father the principal caregiver. He'd had a supposed back injury and stopped working when he was 25. The daughters never told anyone about the abuse, and their mother did nothing to stop it.

I was still somewhat unconvinced. I had taken sociology courses at Miami University, one series entitled Social Deviance. An interesting area of study was incest, which I'd assumed had run its course by this day and age. But the professor revealed that it was not limited to the southern portion of the United States; it was found everywhere within all socioeconomic levels—generally in remote areas where houses lay far apart.

At this father's visitation, his sister was standing in the coffee lounge, waiting for immediate family members to finish their private time with him. I commented that it sounded as if the daughters were having a tough time of it. The woman asked if we could speak privately. We stepped outside, and she began to describe a litany of events. The oldest daughter, who now stood away from her father's casket and showed no emotion, originally endured the abuse, but married at age 17 and left home. This daughter knew the fate awaiting her younger sisters. She tried to warn them and even confronted her mother, to no avail. The mother simply responded that she was lucky to have any man at all in her life. The father's sister eventually suspected foul play and called the police, but each of the daughters lied and said nothing of the sort was occurring.

The sister had come to the visitation only to make certain that her brother was truly dead. She described him as an evil man who had destroyed the lives of all four of his girls. The three children her brother had incestuously sired had been given up for adoption, but the women were now attempting to get them back. This whole sordid mess made me wonder why three adults would grieve so hard for someone who had treated them so poorly and why a death which should rightfully end a reign of terror merely guaranteed that it would continue in another form.

And...

My son and I arrived at a beautiful two-story home in an upscale subdivision to remove the body of a young wife, a cancer victim. Bicycles, big wheels and assorted balls scattered about the carefully manicured lawn told us that this was a tragic case indeed. Three towheaded little boys, ages four, seven and ten, had lost their mother.

We entered the front door and were greeted by the bereaved husband, a red-eyed man of 40. He directed us to the first-floor bedroom, and on the way down the hall we spotted various family portraits of a beautiful blonde woman, her handsome husband and their three sons, all smiling at different stages of life.

Entering the bedroom, we were presented with a vision of sadness—the deceased young woman, still in her bed, surrounded by her mother and her children, each tenderly caressing her, the boys stroking their mother's arms and legs. Their father escorted them out of the room so that we could prepare for her removal. This once-lovely woman had been reduced by cancer to a shell of herself, with sunken, dark eyes, temples depressed from severe weight loss and limbs as thin as sticks.

We carefully carried her into the waiting hearse, and I consulted with the husband regarding burial plans. As we talked, the ten-year-old looked up at me and said, "Mister, I don't want my mom to be dead."

At the visitation two days later, I watched with great sadness as the devastated family arrived. Then the husband and three stairstep little boys stood before the young mother's casket, all wracked with grief. Usually, children of that age are easily bored and restless. But throughout the evening, these boys stood near their father, accepting hugs from relatives, yet all the while stealing glances toward their casketed mother, who had been amazingly restored to her original beauty, looking healthy again, dressed in her favorite skirt and top, her hair styled just like they remembered.

The father wrote me a kind letter a few weeks later that confirmed what I had been thinking. He thanked me over and over for making his wife and the boys' mother look so pretty for her visitation and funeral.

"Cowards die many times before their deaths," said Shakespeare. "The valiant never taste of death but once." However poetic that may be, it misses the mark. No matter how loving, courageous or strong we are, we all taste death many times; in fact, each time we lose a loved one. Nothing can spare us; nothing can prepare us. We have no idea how we'll respond.

Some of us find ourselves more stoic than others. Some stand straight. Others crumple. Some recover in time. Others never do. Some skate to the very brink of madness and then miraculously resurrect themselves. Others fall off the edge and don't come back.

Death unmasks us all. It reveals who we really are.

ᔕ T W O ᔐ

"Does This Mean You'll See Me Naked?"

*People's most common fear regarding
funerals, body art, final requests
and oddest casket inclusions*

Yes, it does mean precisely that. The funeral director who prepares your body for a final viewing will invariably at some point need to remove your clothing. So, yes. You will be naked.

But you'd be amazed at how many times I've been asked that question—and how often, when people voice their fears regarding death, that issue comes up. What is this hang-up people have about nudity? Some of my closest friends have expressed reservations in letting me handle their funerals because of it; even my own sister has mentioned it!

I have repeatedly assured everyone that as a professional I have no sexual interest whatsoever in dead bodies—male or female—particularly family members and friends. Any loved one reposing upon my embalming table is someone's mother, father, sister, brother, daughter, son or grandparent and is reverently and respectfully cared for in a totally businesslike manner. Only a sick mind would interpret or insinuate anything else.

Furthermore, preparation room decorum has always been maintained wherever I have worked. All of my coworkers have been men, and in my opinion, men are all pretty much Mama's boys. A great deal of respect is therefore reserved for deceased women. Any little old lady reminds them of their own beloved grandmothers; a middle-aged female might be the same age as their mothers. And in the case of a deceased little girl, all of us are instantly transformed into protective father figures, feeling intense sorrow right along with the family and sometimes even blubbering tears as we work.

There have obviously been cases involving improprieties in funeral home settings, just as there have been in gynecologists' exam rooms, but such incidents are few and far between. I have never heard of a single case of a male funeral home employee raping or having other inappropriate physical contact with a female decedent. I have, however, heard some sordid tales involving homosexual personnel. One infamous case involved a well-known funeral home up north. The owner professed to be a progressive employer and had no problem with hiring openly gay directors, even touting his equal-opportunity mindset in the local and national news media. He was hailed by the press as a standup, tolerant individual, not at all fearful of what the public might think.

Alas, one day a floral delivery person happened to pass the open preparation room door and encountered a live male engaged in a horrific act with a dead one. The incident was reported to the funeral home owner, whereupon he decided to go public. His news slant was that his attempt at accepting gay employees had back-fired, he was very sorry that such a heinous act had taken place, and he hoped that viewers and readers would not blame him for trying to be open-minded.

Many years ago I worked at a home with a man who eagerly reported for work each morning and then made a mad dash to the preparation room to see if there had been any new calls over-night—supposedly to see if the recently deceased were known to him personally. If so, he was on the horn immediately to report those deaths to his wife and other acquaintances.

But he also made a habit of lifting the sheets covering deceased women so that he could gaze at their private areas. When I ques-tioned him one day, he responded that he was merely looking for a toe tag to determine identity. "The tag is not in her crotch," I told him. He sheepishly left. But when the same incident occurred again the next morning, I reported him to my immediate supervi-sor. The man was fired on the spot, and rightfully so.

But that doesn't mean that we funeral directors don't occasion-ally marvel at the physical oddities we encounter. As a college student working in the county morgue, I saw several decedents whose attributes were...well, noteworthy. Some took the form of off-the-wall embellishments.

A Navy man lay upon the table one morning sporting tattoos over nearly every inch of his body, save for his hands and face. His chest was festooned with a detailed battleship, complete with billowing smokestacks. On his back from neck to buttocks was an intricately drawn butterfly. Around his neck was a broken line with the words "CUT HERE" in bold letters. The stereotypical "MOM" was emblazoned on each bicep, and on each forearm was a buxom lady, each one naked and well-endowed. Drawn on each leg from groin to ankle were hissing snakes with open mouths and forked tongues. And of course, the prerequisite L-O-V-E on his four left fingers and H-A-T-E on the four right ones. (All such body art is considered a distinguishing mark and is therefore noted and photographed.)

I entered the morgue one day to find the coroner holding a magnifying glass to the private parts of a naked man. As I stood next to the body, the coroner handed me the glass and told me to check out the head of this man's penis. In full detail was a drawing of a housefly.

A few months later the magnifier was utilized again to observe another penis tattoo, reading, "Cherry Buster." (I had to wonder just how drunk that person must have been.) But perhaps the finest job I have seen to date is a red-and-white barber pole design, no doubt meant to resemble a candy cane.

Tattoos on deceased women are usually more sedate—flowers, butterflies and the occasional Harley-Davidson insignia. However, I've also encountered "Jimmy's Toys" emblazoned above a woman's ample breasts, "Honey Pot," complete with an elaborate arrow directing the viewer to the vaginal area, and most incredibly, "Deliveries in Rear," inscribed just above a young lady's buttocks.

The coroner and the pathologist of the day used a standard comment upon encountering a deceased man who was endowed with a large penis: "This man will be sorely missed by his wife." Or, if the decedent was not so well-endowed: "I can certainly relate to his situation," followed by raucous laughter. Or, in the case of a large-breasted deceased female, "Her husband is sure gonna miss those." After a few years it continually amazed me that physicians could never come up with better one-liners.

Back then there were not many piercings of note, unlike today. Now men have rings attached to their penises and scrota, women have rings in their clitorises, and both males and females sport nipple rings. Among the more elaborate piercings was a young woman with both nipples and her clitoris pierced and all three connected. A gold chain attached to her nipples hung downward in a U-shape across her chest with another chain attaching the center of the nipple chain to the ring located between her legs. When her mother asked me for any jewelry her daughter might have been wearing, I nervously explained my findings. Although upset, she graciously accepted the items following the funeral.

In my business, prurience, or at least the suggestion of it, seems to be an ongoing issue. I once prearranged the funeral services of a man who insisted that he be placed in his casket completely naked and face down. At first I assumed that this was his interpretation of the old cliché, "Lay me out face down and naked, so the whole world can kiss my ass."

However, his explanation was far less dramatic than that. He'd always slept on his stomach and in the nude, he said, and he desired to be positioned that very way for burial. Also, his casket should be closed, for obvious reasons. I drew red asterisks all over the front of his prearrangement sheet, so that in case I was away when this gentleman passed on, others could be made aware of his wishes.

When he died two years later, I informed his daughter of his request, and she readily agreed to it. I placed the man on a dressing table, covered him with a sheet and then allowed the daughter to view her father and say goodbye before proceeding with the aforementioned arrangements.

Many family members have expressed to me that their deceased loved one would have enjoyed a less-than-traditional send off—more of a party atmosphere than the normal visitation and ceremony complete with traditional hymns and a consoling sermon from a man of the cloth. Although many mention a desire to do something different, I can think of very few who have actually carried out such a plan.

Twenty years ago I arranged for a visitation and service to be held in the social room of an exclusive retirement center. In 1985 this facility was ahead of its time, without peer. Separate condominium-like housing was available for those who were still active and could drive their own cars, assisted living areas were for those less ambulatory, and finally, a nursing home setting was for those who had progressed further toward being bedfast. The gentleman who had passed away was a wealthy business owner. His three grown children applauded his zest for life and preference for the finer trappings. His oldest son told me that his father always wanted to have a send off that involved his Dixieland band mates with whom he had played for many years. They'd marched on the field at Cincinnati Reds and Bengals games, and the group, although elderly, had remained quite close.

So the social room at the retirement community was bedecked not with black bunting, but with bright green ribbons and noise-makers normally reserved for New Year's Eve. The kitchen staff strolled around with serving trays, offering finger food and alcoholic beverages. I stood at the room's rear, pleased by what I observed—folks of all ages eating, drinking and toasting the deceased. Here was the life of the party, the one they'd all come to honor, lying in a solid bronze casket, dressed in a pair of black tuxedo trousers, a white ruffled shirt, green satin bow tie and a red-and-white striped sport jacket. His band mates were off to one side loudly playing "Sweet Georgia Brown" and having the time of their lives. When the band took a break, they all congregated at their late friend's casket, each tipping a glass in his honor.

The deceased man had left behind a wife and a wealth of memories, especially their annual trip to Hawaii. At the funeral the next day, in recognition of his love for our 50th state, I was asked to play the music of Don Ho. His favorite song? "Tiny Bubbles." Everyone in attendance was handed a small bottle of soap bubbles and the obligatory wand. As each mourner and family member passed the casket, a bubbly tribute was administered, complete with that song wafting in the background.

In other cases, whether fueled by alcohol or drug consumption or just plain ignorance, some associates of the deceased attempt to honor certain requests without considering the presence and possible opposition of family members. A motorcycle gang approached me at a visitation one evening and ordered me to take their late friend out of his casket and place him onto a chapel sofa so that he would appear to be relaxing with his buddies. I refused—and amazingly had to explain to this band of drunks that perhaps the man's parents and grandparents might take offense. The group's mouthpiece adamantly claimed that the deceased had always insisted that he did not want to be in a casket for his visitation, so could I please place him on the couch immediately? After a few more minutes of explanations, the others finally conceded my point, apparently realizing how disrespectful such a move would have been.

A young man killed in an auto accident reposed in his casket, with gospel hymns playing softly in the background. His parents were very religious and appreciated the solemnity of Christian music for a church-like atmosphere. But the decedent's hoodlum friends requested that I turn off those selections and play instead the rap CDs they had brought along. I looked over the cases and discovered that these talentless ramblings contained extremely explicit, profane and sexually degrading lyrics, obviously inappropriate for a funeral. I showed the CDs to the parents, and to my surprise, and they said to go ahead and play them.

Well, after about three minutes into the first selection, the father frantically begged me to go back to the hymns. He and his family had probably never heard the bittersweet recollections of a "ho" shaking "the junk in her trunk" and feverishly fondling many male appendages until they "shot their spunk."

When a fun-loving 70-year-old attorney died, his widow expressed to me his desire to have no minister present. One of her late husband's law firm partners would officiate at the funeral instead. Once everyone was seated in the chapel, I escorted the speaker to the podium, noting that he had clearly had a few too many martinis. Not overly concerned, though, I took my position outside the chapel doors to watch the ceremony on a closed circuit television screen.

What I saw and heard was most amazing. This fellow began the ceremony with offensive jokes about Jews, blacks, homosexuals and Mexicans with a comic styling that rivaled even today's standup comedians. It turned out that this was the daily water cooler banter of the deceased and his colleagues; therefore, such material was deemed perfectly appropriate for his funeral. The widow did not even seem offended. Quite a few attendees, however, succumbed to embarrassment and departed, red-faced, via the rear chapel door. Many more left in disgust as the speaker began an x-rated appreciation of various female attributes.

Honoring last requests is generally a simple matter of inclusion. Over the years I have placed a myriad of items inside caskets—including fishing rods, a bow and arrow, golf clubs (sometimes a whole set), golf balls, basketballs, autographed baseballs, baseball gloves and other sports memorabilia, along with complete baseball, football and basketball uniforms. Also, unloaded handguns, rifles and shotguns—sometimes because the deceased was an avid hunter, but just as often because someone apparently didn't want certain family members to take possession of those weapons.

I've included playing cards, bingo cards, lucky pennies, room keys from hotels in Las Vegas and other destinations, cigarettes, marijuana joints, pet rocks, favorite books, a tape recorder, a glass eye, sexual devices, jewelry (some expensive, some not), apples, oranges, buckeyes, walnuts, photographs, leaf collections, coin collections, *Penthouse* and *Playboy* magazines (once, an entire collection) and occasionally even one of the racier publications.

Then there are the dead animals—cremated remains of beloved dogs and cats or the recently euthanized dog, which is placed in a plastic bag and laid at the feet of the deceased.

One recent casket-depositing incident caused quite a furor. The late gentleman was thrice-married and divorced, and all three of his ex-spouses insisted on attending the services. But his current female companion abruptly requested that I remove one of those ex-wives from the funeral home as soon as possible. "Why?" I inquired. She informed me that the woman had just peeled off her panties and placed them in her late ex-husband's hand.

In another less lurid case, an elderly woman's grown children arrived to arrange her memorial service. They commented that they were glad I was being paid in full "up front." My puzzled look prompted one daughter to ask me to look through the bag where

I had already deposited her mother's clothing and find her bras-siere. I did—and discovered that inside the left cup was a sewn-in pocket containing $6000. The daughter laughed and said that her mom always insisted on having her funeral money on her person at all times.

An elderly gentleman friend contacted me when his wife passed away. After the service and with the room empty of mourners, he and I approached the casket. He then handed me a $50 bill and requested that I slip it into his wife's bra. Apparently it was a tradition of sorts—whenever she went someplace without him, he would playfully slip $50 into her bra so she would always have some money with her.

This time would be no exception.

~ T H R E E ~

"Death by Defecation"

*Removal of dead bodies, hoisting the
morbidly obese and why so many people
die while sitting on the toilet*

In most cases, the deceased human body is not the most pleasant sight to behold. Immediately after death many changes begin to take place: discoloration, bowel and bladder evacuations, drainage from the mouth and nose. As previously mentioned, anyone who finds such a presentation sexy is one very deranged individual.

Only once can I recall a time when a dead body was actually beautiful. On Christmas Day, 1978, I was called to a newly constructed apartment complex to remove a 24-year-old suicide victim. A young woman was apparently distraught over a recent breakup with her boyfriend and had hung herself in a clothes closet.

This was long before CSI, Cold Case Files and Drs. Henry Lee and Michael Baden. So the responding life squad personnel cut the woman down and then laid her on her bed, coincidentally just as a funeral director would—on her back, a pillow under her head, legs together and hands across her abdomen, left over right.

The coroner was called and did not respond—it was 1978, remember—to an apparent suicide. He simply phoned me and verbally released the body. Since there would be no autopsy, I could make the removal immediately.

The figure lying on the bed was at first breathtaking. This woman resembled Marilyn Monroe, from her bleached blonde hair to her huge bust. Those breasts struck me visually, due to the fact that they protruded straight upward from her chest like twin Mt. Fujis. No droop to one side, as is normal in death or even when a woman is lying on her back. I understood why no sheet covered her. Life squad personnel and the police photographer were as utterly stunned as I was.

The only other woman in the room was a paramedic. She touched and testified that those breasts were indeed not God-given, but saline-inflated implants. I had never heard of such a thing. By 1970s standards this young lady was something of a trendsetter, a precursor to modern plastic surgery.

Unfortunately, a closer examination of her body revealed the same damning influences of death—her mouth and nose were full of foamy lung material, a deep, ear-to-ear gash reddened under her chin from her ligature of choice (a Venetian blind cord), and the increasingly pungent odor of body wastes filled the room. So much for beauty. So much for leaving, as actor John Derek said in the film "Knock On Any Door," a good-looking corpse. Within moments, that's a virtual impossibility.

A Vietnam veteran, found dead and naked in a motel room that same year, left me with another lasting visual image. I arrived at the scene to find a legless man in bed with his neck still noosed, tied to the steel headboard. This turned out to be another learning experience offered by the kindly, elderly county coroner.

It seems that the deceased was engaging in masturbation, and with the rope knotted tightly around his neck, he could achieve a heightened orgasmic experience by releasing the ligature at just the right moment. Unfortunately, he'd held the ligature in place too long and too tightly and had strangled himself. As the coroner explained this, I stood in perplexed amazement. Apparently I'd led a pretty sheltered life.

Another great visual occurred when I filed the man's death certificate. The coroner had listed the cause as strangulation—as a consequence of "a sexual misadventure." When the upstanding Christian ladies at the health department spotted the coroner's notation, the busybody mode took over, and they demanded to know what that meant. When I defined it for them, I was momentarily concerned that smelling salts might be necessary to rouse them from their horrified swoons.

I learned another valuable lesson once when removing a nude, deceased man from his second-floor bathroom: There are never enough sheets on a mortuary cot. The man in question had just drawn a bath and was sitting on the toilet. His death had occurred while he was still on the commode—which is actually a very common place for a person's demise.

My assistant and I draped a bed sheet across the bathroom floor, then placed the decedent on the sheet and wrapped it around him. We had left our mortuary cot at the foot of the stairs near the front door, since it was not possible to carry it up to the bathroom. We began to hoist the decedent to move him downstairs. My assistant's left arm was positioned under the nape of the man's neck to support his head. His right arm was under the small of his back. I had placed my left arm there too, with my right arm under his knees.

As we made our descent down the stairs, I felt a warm sensation at about thigh level on my pants leg, followed by more warmth on the top of my right foot, accompanied by a familiar odor. I strained against the weight in my arms in an attempt to discover the source. Just as I suspected, the decedent's bowels had given way in a shower of feces that trailed all the way down the carpeted steps and all over our pants and feet.

After placing the decedent on the mortuary cot, I asked the family if I might use their telephone. I called several carpet-cleaning companies, ultimately reaching one that would come to this residence right away.

Of course I paid the carpet cleaner myself, still resplendent in my odiferous attire. But from then on, I always made certain I brought an extra three or four sheets along with the cot. If we had wrapped the man in several sheets, rather than just one, the offensive problem would have easily been contained within the linens. And in most situations, the deceased is normally wearing some sort of clothing, at least pajamas or underwear.

Still, a house call (when death occurs at a private residence) tests the strength and sometimes the ingenuity of those making the removal. A ranch-style home or any residence where the deceased is located on ground-level is a huge plus. In at least half the cases encountered, however, hopes are dashed when we learn the person we must remove is lying in a bedroom on a second or third floor.

New home construction considers not the lowly funeral director. Wide doorways and high-ceilinged atriums in the living areas often give way to narrow upstairs hallways and doorways barely wide enough for a mortuary cot, let alone the ambulance version. People should keep that in mind, since they're likely to need ambulances long before they need funeral directors.

Long ago, when I was a young and foolish teenager, I assisted my older brother, then also a budding director, on several occasions to run ambulance calls and make removals. One morning we were called to the home of a wealthy family. The homeowner's drunken, black-sheep of a brother had died on his mansion's third floor. So we left our cot near the front door and then clambered up the steps to survey the situation. We had brought with us a device called a litter, which is basically three steel poles supporting a thick canvas sheet. It's handily collapsible, so it can be left on the mortuary cot for quick usage as needed.

Entering the room, we discovered the 350-pound decedent supine on the hardwood floor, clad only in jockey shorts and a t-shirt—which was thoroughly soaked in vomit, with stomach contents puddling an outline around the entire body. In all of my fifteen years I had never witnessed such a thing and was on the verge of involuntarily giving up the ham sandwich I had consumed only a half hour earlier.

We placed the litter on the floor next to the deceased, and my older, wiser brother began to rattle off the game plan: I was to simultaneously take hold of the late gentleman's thin t-shirt and the waistband of his jockey shorts and then turn his body toward myself as my brother pushed the litter beneath him. A good-sounding plan—except that I was barely able to budge him. Plan

B entailed both of us lifting this man onto the litter by brute force. Again, I was to grasp the t-shirt and my brother the waistband.

But this plan too went awry as the thin, emesis-soaked shirt slipped from my grasp, and the deceased hit the hardwood floor with a resounding thud. Family members downstairs no doubt heard the commotion, but we hoped they thought we had knocked over a chair. Immaturity ruled as both my brother and I nearly collapsed in fits of muffled laughter, to the point that both of our young faces were red with shame.

On our second try we were finally able to position the deceased onto the litter, cover him and then make our lumbering way down the steps to the waiting cot. Our faces still red, we prayed that the family would assume a strenuous trek down a flight of stairs with a 350-pound man in tow was the source of our breathlessness.

Several years ago I was called to the residence of a deceased 35-year-old female who weighed 660 pounds. Luckily, the local fire department was already at the scene, where the firefighters had dealt with this lady's medical problems before and understood the inherent problems in transporting her. She was found face-up in bed, the construction of which was quite an engineering marvel.

Two twin-sized mattresses rested on two-inch sheets of plywood which had been glued together for more strength. The reinforced plywood sheets were then supported at each corner by concrete blocks stacked on top of each other. After reviewing the situation, I took the mortuary cot out of the hearse and left it in her front yard. There would be no way to fit her onto something that was only 22 inches wide. The life squad personnel and I pondered our dilemma for a few moments until I came up with the plan of the century. I drove to a nearby hardware store and purchased a large canvas tarpaulin.

The tarp was spread out on the floor next to the woman's bed. Seven men assisted me in grasping the bed linens beneath her and gently pulling her onto the waiting tarp. The hearse door was opened, and with four of us on each side, we gripped the tarp and then baby-stepped her to the front door and into the waiting car.

It was the first time I had ever placed a body directly on the floor of a hearse, and there was still very little room to spare. I asked the life squad personnel to follow me back to the funeral home so they could assist in transferring her into the building. Since the decedent was 43 inches wide, she couldn't possibly fit onto a standard embalming table. So I placed two tables side-by-side and latched them together at the legs with nylon rope. We eight pallbearers again baby-stepped the tarp with its cargo into the funeral home, down a short hallway and into the preparation room. Then, after a brief rest, we counted to three and hoisted the decedent onto the two conjoined embalming tables.

Later, since I could not hold the mass of fatty tissue away from her neck in order to locate the carotid artery or jugular vein, I opted for finding and raising the right femoral artery and vein, located at the upper thigh near the groin. After making the femoral incision, I had to ask an assistant to physically hold the incision open with his hands and some strategically placed duct tape. I was nearly up to my elbow in fatty tissue before finally delving deep enough into the femoral space to locate the selected vessels.

Arterially embalming a normal decedent of average weight usually consumes from three to five gallons of formaldehyde-based chemical. In this case I injected fourteen gallons through the decedent's arterial system before I finally starting recognizing some positive results.

After receiving her burial clothing the next day, I pondered the sheer size of the black dress I was instructed to place upon her. My wife styled her hair, I applied cosmetics, and then we awaited the arrival of my seven assistants to move the lady into her substantial casket. I had ordered a custom-made 45" wide 18-gauge steel version which had been delivered within two days.

The next hurdle was coming up with a proper device on which to place the casket. A standard bier, a wooden pedestal-like device on wheels, would not be stout enough to support such massive weight. I called around to inquire the price of having a special bier constructed on short notice—to no avail. During one fruitless call, however, a gentleman referred me to a welding shop known to have rolling carts on which equipment was mounted. The owner invited me to come over and take a look at a steel cart which also sported heavy-duty steel wheels. He then agreed to deliver the cart to me, and after a good scrubbing and taping a black bunting around the top edge, it appeared to be perfectly serviceable.

Throughout this entire ordeal, I made one serious blunder: I decided to place the huge casket on the floor of the preparation room and then removed the lid, so that we could get around both sides as we lifted it. Removing the lid was an excellent idea. Laying the casket on the preparation room floor was not. The tarp had been left underneath it the whole time and was thoroughly cleaned after the embalming process. Thank goodness—because the tarp again needed to be our lifting leverage.

So we hoisted the large decedent into her huge casket and positioned her as well as possible so she would look comfortable in her repose. But suddenly the reality of my blunder sank in to all assembled. We would need to lift her again—this time with the added weight of the casket in which she was lying! I apologized to my hoisting partners, admitted that I should have placed the empty casket into position on the welding cart and then situated the decedent. I also vowed never to make such a mistake again.

Since a 43-inch wide casket will not fit into a hearse, a standard burial vault or standard grave, I had to devise a mode of transportation to the cemetery and then arrange for oversize accommodations once there. The burial vault company offered their flatbed truck, which was also equipped with a hydraulic crane, to be used as a hearse. Following the funeral, the vault truck was backed up to the chapel door, and two canvas strap slings were slid underneath the casket. With little strain, the hydraulic lift gently swooped the casket onto the truck for its short journey to the cemetery.

I'm sure the sight of a white Ford flatbed vault truck with a very large blue casket on the back leading a funeral procession down the street is one not seen very often. Arriving at the cemetery, I noticed that an inordinate number of gawkers had staked their claims near the grave site to catch a glimpse of what they had heard was a very large casketed woman.

The bottom part of the vault waited in a grave that was twice the normal size. The vault company also made concrete septic tanks, so with such a large grave opening, an actual septic tank was utilized. For the first time in my career, I witnessed a graveside ceremony by standing next to a minister and a vault truck, with the honored decedent resting on the truck's bed, rather than on a lowering device above the open grave.

This visitation and funeral service were otherwise attended by some of the most morbidly obese people I had ever seen. The only explanation I can summon is that perhaps they all belonged to the same support group. Gathered family members and other mourners refused to leave the cemetery until their loved one was safely lowered. The canvas slings were attached to the steel ring of the crane's boom. With a twist of a lever, the large casket was raised and then gently cranked downward into its final resting place.

A house call removing a decedent from a private residence as opposed to a medical facility often involves entry into that person's bathroom. I used to be dumbfounded by such scenarios. However, an obvious case can be made in that the elderly sometimes experience difficulty with their bowel movements, and the inherent strain may well be a contributing factor in their deaths. We call it "death by defecation."

Many years ago I was summoned to a residence by the county coroner. As I wrote down the street and house number, it sounded very familiar. Once I turned onto the street, I realized that I was on my way to the home of a kindly old minister friend. Due to his many ailments, over the years I had driven to his house several times to take him to the funeral home to preside over services.

As I pulled in front this time, an ambulance was parked nearby. EMTs and two police officers stood on the minister's porch smoking cigarettes, waiting for me to arrive. Everybody smoked back then, so we all lit up and discussed our plan for removing the body. But the assembled group appeared to be sizing me up. I quickly discovered why. It seems that my minister friend had expired while perched on the commode, and he had subsequently slumped against the door of the tiny bathroom, his full weight pressing it closed.

We all ventured inside to allow me to survey the situation and to hear my expert evaluation of possible procedures. The EMTs and police officers decided that since I was the skinniest one present and familiar with the decedent, then I should be the one to climb inside a small window, squeeze my way into the tiny bathroom, move the man away from the interior door and thus allow for proper removal.

I took off my fairly new double-knit suit coat and with some assistance delivered myself into the bathroom via a window never designed for a 6'3" man. In those days I was at least agile enough to stick my left leg into the room first, followed by swinging my right and then standing upright without even banging my head on the upper sill.

I was certainly saddened to see my friend deceased—but also to encounter him in such an immodest state. Perhaps most poignant was the *Newsweek* magazine, still clutched by a motionless right hand. I have since removed many decedents from bathrooms, more often lying on the floor. But it still remains oddly common to have to pluck that person from atop a commode and then place him on a mortuary cot.

∽ F O U R ∾

"She's Gonna Get Up...She's Gonna Get Up..."

*Grief, denial and parents who endure
the horror of losing their children*

The one common denominator among living things is that we all die—as does everyone we love. Yet few of us seem emotionally equipped to deal with it when it happens. Grief sideswipes us and then knocks us to the ground like some speeding, out-of-control car. No matter how well we accept the many other logical laws of nature, we always manage to claim we didn't see this one coming.

I cried at my own mother's death—and then eventually became resigned that her spirit was in a far better place. Since she saw to it that my siblings and I attended Sunday school and church from age three until past high school, exposure to those many sermons at Front Street Presbyterian Church cemented my belief that we sit at the right hand of God after death. When my mother passed, therefore, I felt somewhat comforted by recalling those streets of gold, walls of jasper and gates of pearl. No more suffering, no more pain, no need for doctors, no need for undertakers... My mother had no doubt earned her heavenly reward.

I still feel secure in that belief, even when the pain of separation gnaws. I rarely visit her grave site, because I know that she is not really there––however, when I do go, I feel a lump in my throat, and I can smile as I ponder the huge and lasting impact of her life here on earth.

Others handle things quite differently. A 30-year-old NASCAR fan's monument is decorated with Matchbox cars. His wife and his mother visit regularly. They sit together on a Jeff Gordon blanket. They stay a long time.

For some reason, major holidays are hugely represented at cemeteries. Grave sites are often festooned with "Happy New Year" noise-makers in January, heart-shaped red balloons in February, green derby hats in March, Easter egg trees in April. I have seen witches on broomsticks and pumpkins of all sizes in October, cornucopia in November. And in December there are more Christmas trees than one can count, some equipped with battery-powered lights, garlands, icicles and even small, beautifully wrapped presents.

I have often wondered why survivors go to such lengths. Is it because the deceased loved the holidays? Or does the family want to include him or her in their merrymaking? Such displays may look garish to observers, yet they obviously provide some degree of comfort, or people wouldn't do it. Grief is an intensely personal journey. Each of us handles it in our own way. Baseball-great Joe DiMaggio was known to have sent fresh bouquets of red roses twice each week since 1962 to the crypt of his beloved former wife, Marilyn Monroe. The only thing that finally stopped him was his own demise in 1999.

There is probably no more heartbreaking human tragedy than for a parent to lose a child to death. I have no idea what that feels like, and I obviously hope and pray that I never do. With over 30 years in this profession, I still cannot help becoming teary-eyed at the sight of any parent, wild with grief, standing over the casket of a recently deceased child, young or old.

A divorced 45-year-old woman wailed and sobbed over her 22-year-old daughter, the victim of a sickening auto accident. The girl had been riding with an inebriated male friend who ran the car off the roadway and into a strand of trees. The impact ejected both from the vehicle. The male was thrown clear and landed softly in the confines of a freshly plowed farmer's field. But the girl flipped in midair and was hurled back-first into a century-old tree trunk. That trajectory and the speed of impact tore her heart from its moorings, causing death in approximately 90 seconds—enough time to lose the volume of blood required for life to be sustained.

Except for a few minor cuts on her face from exiting through the windshield, this 22-year-old was very viewable. After filling the cuts with wax, followed by some overlaid Mary Kay cosmetics, she was easily restored to her former lifelike appearance. When I escorted the mother of this precious child into the funeral home chapel, I could feel her knees buckling and her whole body begin to tremble. She asked for a chair so that she might sit in front of her daughter's casket. But after a few moments of silence, she began what sounded like a chant. "She's gonna get up, she's gonna get up," was recited over and over, sometimes increasing in volume, as if in an attempt to summon the Lord above to again breathe life into her reposing daughter.

A 24-year-old recent college graduate's car slid on a rain-soaked country road and collided with a signpost. Attached to the post was a square piece of yellow steel with the "S" curve warning emblazoned upon it. The square must have been just substantial enough to blast through the windshield and impale the young man directly in the forehead. Death was instantaneous, with tremendous damage done to his face. Then the car careened into a ravine, violently tossing the defenseless occupant to and fro inside, causing even more damage to his lifeless body. When I first saw him, this decedent was broken and torn from nearly head to toe, making for a very time-consuming restoration.

Following the embalming, his limbs were encased in plastic to ensure against leakage, and then the entire body was dressed in a "union suit," a one-piece, formfitting, thick ply plastic garment, which covers the deceased from neck to toes. After filling in the traumatic facial and scalp defects with wax, those areas were then glued and allowed to dry. Due to so many lacerations, this was a three-hour job followed by cosmetics, and in an effort to replace the hair torn away, inserting hair from the back of the head into a wax scalp bed.

After dressing the body and placing him in the casket, I called his parents to see if they wanted a private viewing to approve my considerable efforts. They approached their dead son's casket on tiptoes, as if to be careful not to wake him, wearing that familiar look of devastation that I have witnessed far too many times. As they neared, their output of tears increased—but strangely enough, there was not a howl, nor a wail, nor a scream, nor a sob. The emotional outbursts I had been expecting did not come. Instead, both stood hand-in-hand in front of the casket and stroked their son's hair and cheeks.

I cautioned the mother that his cheeks were freshly waxed and cosmetized, but she didn't heed my warning and continued to stroke her son, eventually rubbing off a lot of my handiwork. She then turned to me and declared that she wanted to see his injuries firsthand. She demanded that I remove the cosmetics and the wax so that she could see for herself the trauma that had caused his death.

At first I was rather irate at such a notion. However, that emotion left me when I remembered that this was her child. How can you say no to the mother who carried him within her body, nourished him at her bosom, changed countless dirty diapers and endured so many sacrifices and setbacks? If she wished to see what had caused his demise, then so be it.

I excused myself from the chapel and gathered up paper towels and a spatula to begin to undo what I had proudly thought was a triumphant restoration. I slowly began to peel off the natural-looking cosmetics and wax, soon revealing a forehead with a wide gash from the right eyebrow upward into the hairline. When the right cheek was uncovered, a shotgun blast pattern appeared, the result of jagged windshield glass against skin.

After a few more moments, luckily for me, the mother asked me to stop. She and her husband had seen enough. Deep down I was glad that I would be able to salvage at least some of my previous efforts. But then I was stunned to hear the mother informing me that she was seriously considering leaving her son unrestored for all to see, especially his friends, so that they might witness what kind of damage could take place as a result of careless, alcohol-impaired driving.

We sometimes assume that a mother's grief at losing an older child might be lessened a bit because an adult child has at least experienced some of what life has to offer. Well, not always. I sat down several years ago with a wealthy 75-year-old widow to arrange services for her 56-year-old alcoholic son. This man had been married and divorced three times, had no children, and was the black sheep of his mother's well-to-do and socially prominent family. This kindly woman was in complete denial concerning her late son's alcoholism, proclaiming that his liver failure was due to other circumstances. After arranging for an evening visitation, a funeral mass the next day, and selecting an expensive solid copper casket, she revealed to me that I should be prepared for a large crowd consisting only of society's upper crust.

She was correct. At the visitation I noticed the parking lot was beginning to swell, accommodating many Cadillacs, Mercedes Benzes and even a Bentley or two. Society's best had indeed arrived to pay their respects to a deceased man whom everyone assumed to be a productive manager with his family's very successful insurance business. In reality this gentleman had spent his days in bars, drinking with unsavory associates and his nights in his family-provided furnished condo. The moment of truth occurred when some of his alcoholic buddies made their way toward the casket, shook hands with the mother and then remarked within earshot of her friends, "Too bad about Jim, but what did you expect? He was a drunk, just like us." The mother attempted to save face by stammering, "You must be thinking of someone else." Surely her momentary embarrassment must have been eclipsed only by the shame she endured upon her next visit to the country club.

A minister's seven-year-old daughter was afflicted with erythro-blastosis and finally succumbed, outliving her doctor's predictions by three years. She died in late November. This charismatic minister and several of his flock waited for me to arrive at the hospital to take his precious child to the funeral home. I placed her little body in the vehicle, and the entire group returned to their cars and then followed me. The pastor-led mourners even accompanied me into the preparation room and assisted me in placing the girl on the table.

My waiting employer and I soon learned that the assembled congregation planned to keep vigil while we embalmed the body. As soon as the prep room doors closed, chanting, wailing and desperate, heartfelt prayers began—and they continued for hours. I wept as I worked, hearing this heartbroken clergyman, his wife and his friends pleading with God to please bring their little girl back to life. Of course it was not to be, and I even felt a little cheated on their behalf that God did not answer prayers so genuinely offered.

After the embalming was completed, we were handed the child's burial clothing, and a casket was hastily selected. This beautiful little girl was cosmetized, dressed and placed in a feminine pink casket, its 54-inch length a sad reminder that this was not some 90-year-old great-grandmother who had lived a long, satisfying life, but a vivid realization of every parent's worst nightmare. The progression of events had certainly been unusual. Leading an unofficial procession from the hospital to the funeral home had occurred before, although not often. Embalming a body, however, while family members and friends waited just outside the door was a first for me, as was dressing and casketing a dead child with the mourners looking on. Still, where grieving loved ones were concerned, I always hesitated to make judgments. Perhaps this was part of their healing process.

But the oddest part was still to come.

Following the funeral, the minister asked us to place his daughter's casketed body in his car. She would lie, he said, near the family fireplace at home, so she could spend Thanksgiving with the rest of the family. And that's exactly what happened. The day after the holiday we were called back to the residence to retrieve the little girl and then conduct a proper funeral service.

A telling opposite took place in the case of a two-year-old child whose parents were estranged, living apart. The child had been in the care of his mother and her new boyfriend, who described the toddler's death as "an accident." When I called the medical examiner's office to arrange for the release of the little body, the morgue secretary asked me if I had children, and I responded affirmatively. She further inquired if any of my children at age two had ever fallen on a vinyl kitchen floor, and if they did, had they died? Of course they had not, and the secretary then rested her case. The coroner ordered an autopsy and was investigating this case as a homicide.

As I placed the cute little scamp on the preparation room table, I immediately recognized the same signs of abuse that I have unfortunately observed far too many times—facial bruising, round bruises on each arm which curiously matched the shape of adult fingertips, and two telling, perfectly round bruise outlines on the chest—about the size of quarters and suspiciously matching the buttons you might see on a child's jumper or bib overalls.

The bruises were covered with makeup, and the child was placed in a 36-inch white fiberglass casket, larger than necessary to accommodate the toys and trinkets that I knew would be placed inside with him. I awaited the family's arrival. The father, grandparents, aunts, uncles and others showed up en masse, and the touchingly familiar cries began. The mother soon arrived with her male friend, and the crowd in the chapel parted to allow her access to her deceased son. All the while those in attendance, myself included, studied her to gauge her reaction. Surprisingly, or perhaps not, there were no tears. She stood over her child and began speaking to him, asking him why he had to die and stating that she was so sorry to have to be in this place. Her male friend never left her side. He followed her around like a lost puppy, I suppose to avoid any conflict with assembled guests, who all assumed he was somehow responsible.

While I was alone with the mother for a few moments, she asked me why there was cosmetic on her son's face. When I explained that the bruising needed to be covered, she acted astonished. She then attempted to explain what had happened; she was supposedly at the store with her mother while her boyfriend was home alone with her child. Upon her return she was confronted by an ambulance in her driveway and her son being rushed outside. He had supposedly fallen over backward from a chair onto a carpeted floor. Then the story changed. It was a hardwood floor. Then it changed again. She didn't really know what had happened, because she was in the bathroom at the time, not out shopping at all.

I'm no detective, but such stories cannot possibly be truthful. It quickly became obvious that she was covering up for her boyfriend. I was puzzled as to why these two were even allowed on the street, since any child's home death is always investigated as a murder. I had to commend the child's father for his restraint. I was personally tempted to allow my old-school neighborhood justice to kick in, take the boyfriend out to the garage, beat him senseless with a baseball bat and then explain to the investigating authorities, "He must have fallen down on the garage floor." But the coward was eventually taken into custody, and from what I have heard since, he will definitely receive his fair reward in prison.

Inmates have children too, and they absolutely despise child killers.

"I Need to Be Up Front; I Was His Favorite Cousin."

*The curious custom of sending flowers
and why some "mourners" behave so badly*

Flowers are a universal expectation when people arrive at a funeral home. The casket spray, for example, is that large "family" piece which adorns the casket lid. Priced between $175 and $350, depending on sizes and types of flowers used, it's a big-ticket item any florist is delighted to provide, hopefully with several matching companion pieces to further set the mood—and spike the tab.

Florists and funeral homes generally enjoy an amicable relationship, since funeral orders comprise the bulk of any florist's business (Valentine's Day, Secretary's Day, Mother's Day and Sweetest Day notwithstanding) and provide a consistent month-to-month cash flow. But some are more principled than others. Competing florists have tried to woo my affection by offering roses to my wife, fruit baskets or a free spray for every large order I provide. The florist's eternal hope is that the funeral home itself will call for flowers, perhaps ask for a casket spray along with its companions, and then simply add those charges to the family's invoice. In other words, he prefers to be kept out of the mix, so he doesn't need to worry about sending a bill and then trying in vain for months to collect on it.

I have actually attempted to place an order on a family's behalf, only to be turned down when I requested that the florist bill the family directly. Other pain-in-the-neck florists are those who call me for funeral information when they could just as easily open a newspaper. If the majority of my business consisted of providing flowers to funeral homes, then I would certainly subscribe to all local papers and scan the obituaries daily. Not only would the visitation and funeral times be quickly confirmed, I could also note the correct spelling of the deceased's name. Families are already upset enough—finding their loved one's name misspelled on a floral sympathy card is just one more painful thorn in their sides.

There are also rude delivery people who enter through the funeral home's front door during services already in progress with a late bouquet, waltz right into the chapel and loudly announce their presence. There is no excuse for this. Most funeral homes have a backdoor flower drop-off which is checked frequently.

As late as the early 1970s, there were far more flowers sent to honor the deceased. Whether he or she was 29 or 99, the chapel was always filled with that fresh, sweet fragrance. We used a panel truck back then (now morphed into a mini van) to transport cemetery pieces to the grave site before the funeral procession arrived—typically, cut flowers arranged in paper mache baskets or plastic buckets, as opposed to the more elaborate (and fragile) live plants, glass vases and dish gardens—and our vehicle was always stuffed to the gills.

Today quantities of bouquets and arrangements sent have been significantly reduced. Friends and even relatives seem to be pooling their resources and going together on a single basket—so instead of one name on the attached card, you now see seven or eight.

The number of deserving charities has also increased dramatically; therefore, folks are wisely donating money in lieu of flowers. There are still a few who give to a charity and also purchase a basket, perhaps so they can point it out to assembled mourners: "Those are the flowers we sent." I can hardly believe, however, the conflicts which can arise over funeral blooms, and they're usually from shirttail relatives or people not even related to the deceased.

On many occasions I have had to physically restrain individuals from snatching up live plants and rose-filled vases while the casket is still proceeding out of the chapel. My duty is to deliver the cemetery pieces first, then later the keepers—healthy plants, vases, silk arrangements and the like—to the family residence. The husband, wife, parents or grown children should rightfully decide what is to be done with them. But when I question a non-relative attempting to carry away a floral piece, I often receive a puzzling response: "These are the flowers from my work, and I want them."

I have unsuccessfully tried to explain, yes, those flowers may have indeed been sent here by your place of employment—but not for your enjoyment. Instead, as an expression of sympathy to the family. I guess I have yet to compose the ideal reprimand, because I'm so often answered with yet another shameless remark.

The funeral procession itself can be an emotional land-mine. It is usually arranged in the order of immediate survivors: First, the spouse. Second, the children. Third, grandchildren, and fourth, brothers and sisters. Fifth, other relatives and friends. Special parking spaces are reserved for the immediate family, with the rest available on a first-come, first-served basis.

Several times each year, conflicts develop over where certain parties should be placed within the procession. I've heard many great territorial claims, most along the lines of, "I need to be up front; I was his favorite cousin," even if it means riding ahead of a son or daughter. I usually compile a passenger car list as part of the funeral arrangement process, with the order clearly approved in advance by the immediate family. When I tell a disgruntled "mourner" that this is in fact the way the family wants the cars lined up, that statement normally quells any disturbance.

The actual funeral procession has become quite an adventure over the years, with passing drivers increasingly preoccupied with their radios, cigarettes and makeup applications—combined with today's even more dangerous pastimes of talking on cell phones and even watching television from behind the wheel.

As the lead car, I have often maneuvered a hearse into an intersection, only to be greeted by angry motorists who give me the finger for holding them up. During mild weather months, with windows open, I've had to listen to some pretty colorful and profane diatribes. The average driver often fails to realize that a funeral procession enjoys the legal right of way and takes precedence over any other vehicle except a lighted emergency one. Failure to yield to a funeral procession is a costly moving violation.

I attempt to give as much instruction as possible beforehand to those participating. I recommend turning headlights on and following the car just ahead as closely as safety permits. "Think of it as a parade," I say. Alas, most procession drivers are either too upset by the circumstances or choose not to listen. They lag far behind, which makes for a dangerous situation when approaching any cross street.

Behavior in general, along with styles of dress at funerals, has recently reached new lows. I suppose this is reflected in other aspects of modern life as well, since even churches now encourage folks to "come as you are," and airline travelers no longer don their Sunday best, not even in first-class. So teenagers will attend funerals wearing rock band-emblazoned t-shirts, cutoff shorts and sandals. Girls float in wearing hip-hugger pants that expose not only their bellies, but also the cracks of their buttocks.

Adults may dress a bit better, but their actions still leave much to be desired. Some who attend visitations stand right outside the funeral home door, venturing inside only for a moment to sign the guest book and make their presences known—but otherwise puff on cigarettes, spit tobacco juice and spew raw profanity accompanied by plenty of raucous laughter. Not exactly a pleasant experience for more respectful mourners who hold their breath as they walk through acrid clouds of smoke, dodge puddles of brown phlegm and close their ears to offensive language.

Rude smokers continually astonish me by flipping cigarette butts into our decorative mulch and onto our pavement, or by stubbing them out in our concrete entryway. I've even seen people emptying their overflowing car ashtrays into the funeral home parking lot.

The elderly funeral director for whom I worked in the 1970s told me that you could always tell the class of people at a visitation by the number standing outside smoking—or by the number who strolled in carrying bottles of soda pop. I now provide coffee and soft drinks at no charge, but at least once a month I kick myself over it. When something is free, there seems to be no regard for the amount consumed. I expect some lack of discretion among children, but I actually have more drink problems with adults. Grown men and women will exit a funeral home with three or four cans of soda tucked under their arms for the ride home.

After questioning a lady about this once, she said she was taking a can home to her mother who couldn't make it to the visitation. And after watching two overweight little boys consume six pops apiece in one evening, I told them that they'd had enough. Their mother overheard and cursed at me for denying her sons the pleasure of a seventh can. I again hearken back to the wisdom of my 1970s employer. He said that if no one set foot in the coffee lounge the entire evening, that was the mark of a classy bunch. That crowd did what they were supposed to do—sign the register, offer words of sympathy to the family, view the deceased and then leave quietly. But when serving and opening one's facility to the public, those from all walks of life (and forms of upbringing) are likely to show up at your door.

One evening I happened upon a woman rummaging through the lounge cupboard.

"What are you looking for?" I asked from the doorway.

She looked up, startled. "Coffee," she responded. "I thought I'd make some."

I gestured toward the freshly brewed pot sitting, still full, in clear view on the counter. But like most people caught in a lie, she became even more defensive.

"Well!" she huffed. "I was only trying to help!"

Yeah. Right.

I'm amazed at the petty thefts that occur. Objects disappear constantly, everything from rolls of toilet paper, entire boxes of tissue (including their decorative plastic covers), scented candles from the women's restroom, ink pens from the register book stand (pens are now attached with a chain), even the silk floral arrangements that adorn our end tables. We now purchase only arrangements too large to fit into any woman's purse.

People also say things inside funeral homes that they would never say anywhere else in polite society. They'll walk up to a casket with the family of the deceased standing nearby and make remarks like, "Gee, Bert sure wasted away to nothing, didn't he?" Or "How did they get Aunt Jean into that casket, with a shoe horn? She sure gained a lot of weight."

That foot-in-mouth syndrome occurs less often when the deceased is elderly. People seem slightly more comfortable in dealing with the death of an aged loved one—who clearly lived a long life, accomplished much and has now gone on to his or her just reward. Otherwise, visitors are so unhinged with the notion of death and the circumstances of their visit that odd utterances just seem to pop out. It's a defense mechanism of sorts, and summoning the right words can be difficult. So I try to give people the benefit of the doubt whenever I hear insensitive comments and spot rude actions. Death is a shock, we don't understand it, and we are never sure exactly what to say to a grieving family. The younger the deceased person, the lower the comfort level. Anyone who dies under age 50 denotes a probable tragedy—a spouse and children left behind, along with many unfulfilled dreams and many stunned friends.

Common sense, however, should prevail. I have heard visitors ask in loud, booming voices how the person died. At the visitation of an auto accident victim, people will inquire if in fact the deceased was decapitated. When a family opts for a closed casket, perhaps because of severe trauma, or because that may have been the deceased's wish, there are those who have the gall to ask why.

Some even leave abruptly, muttering, "If I had known the casket would be closed, I wouldn't have come tonight."

Suicide cases, always jarring, somehow seem to bring out an even darker, crueler mentality. I have overheard utterly classless individuals ask the family how the deceased "did it." Or, "How many pills did she take?" Or, "Did he really put the shotgun right into his mouth?"

Since the place of final disposition is usually the last place where all bereaved family members will gather, that is also the place where family conflicts come to a head. A few years ago I arrived at the cemetery for the burial of the father of two sons. The sons could not stand each other. Neither spoke to the other at the visitation or service. The older, who had arranged for and paid the funeral bill, requested that I give him the guest registration book. But then the younger approached me at the cemetery and demanded it.

When I informed him that it was traditional to present the book to the person who paid, he produced a handgun, pointed it at me and asked for the register book again. I immediately complied with his request and handed it over. I then informed the armed man that I would be happy to return to the funeral home and photocopy the pages for him instead. He agreed, apologized and put away the gun.

A deceased woman was the mother of seven daughters and five sons. Family closeness had been severely tested when the youngest daughter had divorced her husband and then began a new union with a lesbian lover. The evening of the mother's visitation proved to be a strain, with all eleven siblings making derogatory remarks to their sister and to her new love interest.

The tenseness continued the following day during the funeral ceremony. Not only was the tainted daughter not permitted to sit in the front row with her siblings; her oldest sister began making threats to her sister's lover.

We arrived at the cemetery, listened to the minister's words and then proceeded toward our respective vehicles. That's when the fireworks started. The oldest sister strode up to the lesbian lover and attempted to tackle her. But since the lover was bigger and more athletic, she quickly pummeled the sister into submission—to the amazement of the gathered mourners and myself.

One winter day a few years ago, a large crowd gathered at the graveside of a deceased young man who had accidentally overdosed on a variety of painkillers. Before the minister was able to speak, two inebriated females began to argue. One was a former girlfriend, the other, his current one. One accused the other of providing their late lover with the lethal concoction that ultimately took his life. As blows began, it was obvious to both battling parties that neither was particularly accurate with punches. So they both reached down to the snow-covered grass and began to pack snowballs to hurl at each other.

Unfortunately, their aim was off as well, so more than a few bystanders were struck in the crossfire. The minister was so disgusted that he quietly departed, leaving me to say a few words over the deceased man's grave.

A young couple was recently found dead in their home, both victims of a heroin overdose. I had naively assumed that heroin usage was a 1960s relic, but it's unfortunately still common today. This young couple had left behind three elementary school-age children, who were to be cared for by a loving aunt.

At the cemetery for the double burial, another aunt, who must have thought she should have been the designated caregiver, felt compelled to create a scene. Drunk and disorderly, she told anyone who would listen that the deceased couple "got what they deserved" for their constant illegal drug use. Finally another family member asked the aunt to leave. Her response was to get into her car and then, on her way out, ram as many of her family members' vehicles as she could.

Another case involving a husband and wife who had accidentally overdosed on Oxycontins featured an angry confrontation between two feuding relatives who had supplied the couple with their deadly stash. These mental-midget females each accused the other of furnishing the deceased couple with a big bag on the previous night—but before they could agree on the exact timeline, blows were exchanged. One of the brawlers then left the building, only to be followed outside by two other women, who proceeded to beat the first one to a pulp. The scrap was over by the time police arrived, and the two attackers returned inside the chapel to brag loudly about their fist-fighting prowess.

Drug abuse deaths and their commonality have confounded me for years. Not the intentional overdoses, but the accidental overinjestions of methadone, cocaine, meth amphetamines and Oxycontins. The levels of illicit drugs found in a person's system can be shocking, causing me to wonder if certain persons just cannot get enough of the stuff. Birds of a feather flock together, and that cliché is no more apparent than at the funeral services of deceased drug abusers.

Their female friends are easily recognizable—skinny from poor nourishment, unkempt from no longer caring how they look in public or perhaps so stoned that they don't realize how terrible they appear. Other adult mourners are rarely teary-eyed or emotional, perhaps because they understand the inherent risks of such abusive behavior. They may also realize that they could be next. Yet they can't or won't discontinue their lifestyle of choice. In many cases, the deceased leave behind small children, who may well become patrons of public assistance.

Children at funeral homes are always a sticky subject, depending on their ages and maturity levels. We funeral directors don't appreciate being drafted into the roles of baby-sitters, but unfortunately, such is often the case. Four-year-old Jimmy and three-year-old Janie have no business being allowed to roam free and unmonitored in a place filled with distraught, weeping grown-ups—plus, untold opportunities for getting into mischief.

I have seen small children knock over flower vases, push over lamps, yank every tissue out of a box and then toss all of them onto the floor, pull pictures off walls and onto themselves, jump off chairs and couches, remove couch cushions and then hurl them onto the carpet, repeatedly kick walls with their new leather shoes, pitch entire rolls of toilet paper into commodes, turn restroom water faucets on and leave them on, slam doors over and over and rub their dirty fingerprints on walls, molding and door glass. Perhaps worst of all is any mother who thinks it is just so cute when Junior holds the front door open for visitors, thereby letting out the conditioned air and letting in flies and other insects.

Parents, occupied with greeting visitors, can easily fail to keep track of their brood. But I have heard a few declare that they expect my staff (and me!) to watch their children while they speak to relatives. One informed me that I needed to build a playground on the property to keep her children occupied.

I am all for allowing little ones to view and say goodbye to deceased loved ones, but if they are unlikely to remain at their parents' sides or in custody of an older sibling, then they should be left at home.

"Why Would You Want to Hang Out with Dead People?"

*Why burial is the ultimate solution,
how the undertaker's role has evolved,
and why we really are full of it*

Burying a dead human body deep in the ground has always been the best way to rid society of a potentially serious physical and psychological health hazard. Leaving it outdoors to be ravaged by nature's elements is deemed repulsive and disrespectful. The strong stench, the bloating, the rapid liquefaction, the insect and small animal activity, along with rampant bacterial growth and the possibility of disease have all moved us as a decent culture to dispose of our dead as quickly and efficiently as possible. That inevitably means either depositing the body several feet beneath the earth's surface or in a tightly sealed, aboveground crypt.

The unforgettable odor of decomposition has long been recognized by anyone who has ever owned a horse, a cow, a dog or a cat. Upon that animal's death, obvious changes occur. Even Biblical scholars made note of putrefaction: "Jesus lay in the tomb for three days; surely He stinketh." And that Shakespearean scene we all remember from high school where Romeo visits Juliet in her family's mausoleum for one last kiss? No way. Since Juliet wasn't really dead yet, she smelled just fine. But her grandparents' remains would have knocked poor Romeo right out of his socks.

It was a Dr. Thomas Holmes in the 1860s who first conceived the idea of injecting a preservative into the arteries of dead Civil War soldiers so that their bodies could be sent home in a somewhat presentable condition. Unfortunately, arsenic happened to be his liquid of choice, and some of Dr. Holmes' students actually died from exposure to it while administering rudimentary embalmings.

Injecting a preservative chemical into the right femoral artery or right common carotid artery and opening the accompanying vein allowed the blood, a major source of decomposition's odor, to drain out of the body—thus allowing the chemical to react with and preserve or harden the surrounding tissues. Today formaldehyde-based chemicals mixed with water "fix" human tissue to such a state as to allow for funeralization to take place.

Embalming, however, is not forever. Such a procedure merely retards decomposition for a matter of days, perhaps weeks. In time the skin begins to leather and eventually assumes a grayish-brown tint known among funeral directors as "formaldehyde gray."

The services provided by undertakers were humble in their genesis. Two centuries ago they worked primarily as cabinetmakers and proprietors of furniture stores. The deceased's family would often contact the local cabinetmaker to construct a crude coffin— wide at the shoulders and narrow at the hips to accommodate the human form. That human was then placed in the wooden box.

Those of means might request that ice be placed under and alongside the body to slow decomposition and somewhat eliminate the coming odor. But ice was such a luxury in those days that only the well-off could afford it.

Undertakers were also called upon to dig graves. Again, one's financial status determined whether that service could be hired out. Many family members dug the graves of loved ones themselves, usually on their own property, until organized cemeteries became more popular and necessary.

Undertakers soon realized they could make far better livings by caring for the dead than by building furniture. Their roster of services grew and evolved into customarily dressing the deceased for a family's final viewing and arranging for a fine carriage to transport the loved one to the cemetery. Also, coffins could be embellished with quilted linings and brass handles—all for a price. Impressing one's friends and fellow townspeople of one's prominence and standing was an additional motive for sending the deceased out in style with untold finery and craftsmanship. Unfortunately, many an expensive coffin was nastily soiled by the decedent himself, until Dr. Thomas Holmes came along as the father of arterial embalming.

Those cabinetmakers who constructed coffins obviously could not conduct funeral services inside their own buildings. Livery stable operators who provided horses for funeral carriages could offer little better. So what did folks in the late 1800s decide to do? Go to church—always a good place for any gathering of mourners. (The unchurched could opt for graveside-only.) Meanwhile, enterprising undertakers opened storefronts in downtown areas, with their furniture establishments on one side and their funeral parlors right next door. Picture windows facing the street gave passersby an opportunity to view the latest coffins, displayed vertically so that they could inspect the plushest interior options. As more organized and more elaborate funerals came into vogue, undertakers expanded even more by purchasing large, mansion-like homes so that they could live upstairs and conduct business downstairs. The era of family-owned funeral businesses, where owners hoped that their sons would someday carry on the tradition, was born.

When the horseless carriage arrived in the early 1900s, leading undertakers immediately seized advantage. A motorized hearse to carry a casket to the cemetery was a source of immense pride and fueled competitive fires among many funeral parlors. Another potential source of revenue soon galloped into mind: Why not use the hearse for an ambulance on occasions when the funeral business was slow? The infirm could be transported to the hospital for treatment and then return home in a fine conveyance—complete with the undertaker's name emblazoned on that vehicle's sides. When Grandma finally died, which firm do you think was called to conduct her funeral service? Definitely a win-win.

Invalid ambulance services became such a staple in the funeral industry that major hearse manufacturers were soon building what they termed "combinations." A hearse/ambulance on a Cadillac chassis had reversible rollers in the rear casket compartment. The rollers allowed a casket to slide into the rear of the hearse, yet could also be reversed to disappear into the floor so the now-flat compartment could easily accommodate an ambulance cot. Anyone who has ever attended a funeral will instantly recognize the genius behind it.

One funeral home operator acquaintance of mine was exceedingly proud of the fact that for years he ran six ambulances at all times. He even transported accident and cardiac victims in the event that life squads were tied up. But this man and his employees also had an odd habit of photographing the more spectacular and graphic auto accidents, suicides and industrial accidents he attended. The photos were then organized into albums, unmarked except for the years of occurrences and appearing to be just quaint collections with generic flowery motifs or cute animals on the front covers along with the ever-popular "Photo Memories."

One day I observed a woman waiting inside his office. In a moment of boredom, she picked up one of the albums conspicuously arranged year-by-year right on the director's desk. As she began to thumb through it, her eyes widened. Soon she was on her way to the ladies' room to relieve her revolted stomach. When I told the funeral director about it, he was unmoved, in fact, curiously amused.

So why on earth would anyone want to work with dead people in the first place? I have been asked that question more times than I can count.

Actually, working with the deceased is probably the smallest facet of the entire funeralization process. Far more time and attention are spent on the bereaved family. So I'll simply repeat what funeral directors have been telling the public for nearly two hundred years: We provide a very essential and valuable service. In that regard, what I do for a living is a mere sidestep away from practicing medicine, teaching first grade or hoisting a fire hose. All of us are equally devoted to helping people in need.

The older I become, the more I realize how important that role is, especially when I see so much pain in the eyes of surviving family members. My taking charge becomes even more vital when I am acquainted or personally related to the deceased. Once I dealt with the deaths of my classmates' grandparents. Now I am caring for their parents. Although I certainly dislike facing close friends who have lost loved ones, I also know that most are very pleased that their undertaker of choice is someone they know.

I was tested severely, however, in 1992 when my niece, still in her twenties, tragically lost her husband. The two were newlyweds, the handsomest of couples. My niece was summoned to the hospital, unaware that her husband was already dead. She arrived, assuming that he had merely injured himself on the job.

When informed of her husband's death, she was asked which funeral home she preferred. Still devastated, she told the nurse, "You'll have to call my uncle, Bob Webster." Upon my arrival at the hospital, my niece was visibly relieved that a family member would handle things. That tragic death left a mark on me which endures to this day—but although heartbroken, I was glad to offer some small degree of comfort.

The same thoughts returned recently when a 36-year-old son of a close friend died. My friend is an upbeat, caring gentleman who always greets my children with huge, heartfelt bear hugs. Although reluctant to face him at such a horrible time, I was gratified when he told me that he would not have allowed anyone else to handle the funeral arrangements. He was reassured, knowing that I would treat his son and family just as I would my own.

Yet the general public continues to respond to what I do with morbid fascination. Overall, I think I'm a pretty normal guy. I go to parties. I enjoy baseball and backyard barbecuing. I tell lots of corny jokes—just ask my kids. I don't wear a black cape. I don't have fangs or talons.

Privately I believe that hang-ups about funeral directors have much to do with our culture's obsession with youth, beauty, fitness—hence, a total denial of death. Acknowledging that we directors exist and can over time earn substantial livings confronts everyone with the jarring, indisputable evidence that...oh, my gosh! People die!

But anyway, a bit of background.

The greatest influence in my decision to pursue a career in the death care industry was my older brother John. I idolized him. As a fourteen-year-old, when I was still following him around like a puppy dog, he permitted me to join him at his place of employment—a funeral home! Feeling like pretty hot stuff, I hung out with him and his coworkers, even the bosses, and was soon treated just like one of the guys. I was allowed to print memorial folders, wash the big, fine cars and perform the ultimate gofer service, running to the corner grocery for Pepsi-Colas and candy bars. It was my first experience with the hip language of the day: "I'll buy if you'll fly." In other words, if you hike on down to the Handy Pantry and get everyone a Pepsi and a Mounds bar, you'll be rewarded with your own. How cool was that? Only in eighth grade and already accepted by young men.

They seemed to take me under their collective wings and treated me like their own little brother, complete with the requisite name-calling, the degradation of one's mother, the constant punches in the chest and arm, and, of course, getting to hear unending, untrue but nevertheless scintillating tales of sexual conquests.

I knew that spending time in a building specific to the care of the deceased would eventually result in my actually seeing a dead body. Originally repulsed by the idea, once it happened I realized there's nothing more natural than the fact that we are all going to die, some of us sooner than others. My new "siblings" were amazingly gentle with me about it. I had made every attempt to avoid the preparation room during my first few days, categorizing even my own brother as perhaps a slight bit weird to want to work in such a place. So from day one, the guys would try to get me to go into the prep room to either observe an embalming or simply assist in placing a decedent into a casket. My response was, "No, thanks. All of you have to be nuts."

But when the day finally arrived that I was led inside, all present conducted themselves with the utmost solemnity and decorum. I was encouraged to touch the deceased elderly man's embalmed arm, noting the surprising degree of firmness achieved, to gaze upon his dead but incredibly lifelike facial features. I even stood nearby as my new pals dressed him in his Sunday best.

This was a defining moment. I now understood what these people actually did for a living. They cared, really cared for the dead.

Little did I know that soon afterward their immaturity level would take over, and the first of many initiation rituals would begin. I was unceremoniously pushed to the floor, and my peers streaked out, turning off the lights and locking the door. With no windows, this room was as dark as any cave, and I was now imprisoned inside it—with a corpse. The only saving grace was that everyone stood just outside, hooting with uncontrollable laughter. As young as I was, I began to spew forth a tirade of newly coined curse words, compliments of my training by older men. I was soon freed, probably because my real brother figured I'd had enough, and upon my release I was showered with insults questioning my manhood. But a rite of passage had definitely occurred.

John, still my hero, was at first the only reason I kept coming back. Just to to be around him was both inspiring and validating. But when my beloved junior high Latin teacher, a refined lady in her early sixties, discovered that I was "sort of" on the staff at a local funeral home, she grew warm and intrigued and later told my mother that I would someday make a fine, respectable undertaker. She had unfortunately endured the deaths of both of her parents and three siblings in a span of just two years, but had only the best to report concerning her treatment and experiences with their funeralization processes. Since she'd likely never heard of an adolescent boy desiring to become an undertaker rather than a policeman or a fireman, I enjoyed her beaming approval and had to endure many pats on my Brylcreemed head, which resulted in constant ribbing from the other students. Still, the friendly conversations she and I shared became the springboard that finally convinced me of what I wanted to do with my life.

With school in session and basketball to be played, my time at the funeral home was limited mostly to weekends. That was a fun time as well, because in those days there were no answering machines, pagers or cell phones. Funeral home employees took turns staying all night to answer the telephone. When my brother and I took our turn we stayed awake (sleeping was for sissies and overrated anyway), watching All-Night Theater on a tiny black-and-white rabbit-eared television. When a death or ambulance call materialized, two people were required to respond, so someone else had to be called in to man the phones.

Once when we received a late night call, we could find no one to stay. In desperation we reached our father and presented him with two options: Go on the death call, or else remain at the funeral home and catch the phone until we returned with the body. Dear old Dad chose the former, so he and my brother hustled off, while I stayed behind. Unfortunately for Dad, the decedent was a 350-pound lady found on her living room floor. Upon returning, he was aghast and uttered words that would live in our hearts forever: "Don't ever ask me to do that again. I'm better suited as a phone man."

Perhaps the most classic indoctrination I endured was when I was the unwilling participant in a photo op gone awry. Our funeral home owner had always taken pictures of flower baskets delivered and then presented the collections of photos to families as keepsakes. On one particularly slow evening, when we were supposed to be washing cars for the next day's services, a plan was hatched. Let's have the new guy (me) lie down in a casket and take his picture! My brother assured me that it would be absolutely hilarious, so I agreed. I was carefully lifted and then placed inside. But on the way in, I couldn't help noticing that no camera equipment was present. As the double lids were slammed down on me, I heard a crank being inserted into the foot end, the manner in which a casket is sealed closed for eternity. Only my kicking at the interior of a very expensive model saved me from a few more moments of terror. That I was a relatively good sport throughout the ordeal cemented a new found respectability for me among my peers.

After high school I wasn't able to accumulate enough hours at the funeral home to make a decent living, so I set out to secure summer employment. My two sisters were registered nurses at the local Catholic hospital, so I dropped their names on my job application. The human resource director was a former nursing instructor who had taught both of my sisters, loved them dearly and assumed that I must be a similarly astute young person. I described my career goals—to attend Miami University, then the Cincinnati College of Mortuary Science, serve a year's apprenticeship under a licensed embalmer and funeral director, take the state-board examination and then get on with the fulfilling business of caring for the dead. She gave me a puzzled look, wondering briefly what a potential undertaker could possibly do in a hospital setting. Then, brightening, she stated that I would be perfect as an orderly. Even doctors in training, she gushed, had once been young orderlies, and in a teaching hospital, a certain number of autopsies must be performed yearly in order for the hospital to maintain its accreditation—so a future embalmer could be very helpful in the autopsy room.

I listened and nodded as she explained the vast realm of my duties: Maintaining and installing traction devices under the direction of an orthopedic surgeon; catheterizing male patients; prepping (shaving) them prior to surgery. This was the early 1970s. Female nurses were then forbidden to insert catheters into men or shave their private areas, and, of course, males were not permitted to do the same for female patients.

I got the job and to my delight was assigned to work nights, 11 p.m. until 7 a.m. When college started I could work and still attend classes, both full-time. (That's when I discovered again that sleeping is overrated.) My preparation for the funeral business, where being awake and active at 3:00 a.m. is common, had now officially begun.

The catheterization procedure was taught to me by a fellow orderly of ten years' experience. He was a homosexual--my first contact with someone of that persuasion. I found myself ogling the female nurses more demonstratively than ever in his presence just to reassure him that I was not available.

A Foley catheter is needed when the patient either cannot urinate or if urine output must be measured precisely. The procedure initiates by gloving, placing a sterile drape around the pelvic region, swabbing the head of the penis with Betadine (a liquid sterilization agent), covering the end of the catheter tube with KY jelly and slowly inserting the lubricated tube into the penis, past the urethra and into the bladder. A plastic urine collection bag is attached to the catheter tube, and that bag is hung on the patient's bed, visible for the nursing staff to monitor urine output. The catheter tube has an angled connection that is injected with water, which fills a small balloon on the tube, allowing it to remain in place in the bladder. A straight catheter is a tube inserted into the bladder and drained into a small pail positioned between the patient's legs, normally utilized in emergency situations for quick drainage. A Texas catheter is a condom-like device with a drain tube attached, which is connected to a urine collection bag hung on the patient's bed, for cases where the patient is unable to accommodate a tube insertion into the urethra.

My sister Gale was the charge nurse of the surgery floor, and she would summon me on many occasions to perform catheterizations. Once she gleefully instructed me to affix a Texas catheter onto a patient, knowing the difficulty such a procedure presented. It was my first encounter with having to place a condom-like structure on another male. The most trying part was getting the rubber device attached to a flaccid penis. You can imagine the advice the nurses were giving me on possible solutions.

A few months later Gale happily made me the butt of another humorous scenario. I reported to her floor and was instructed to go to room 262 to insert a Foley catheter into the patient. As I made my way down the hall, I distinctly heard the nurses snickering. I looked back and could tell from their reddened, laughing faces that I was about to encounter something out of the ordinary.

I entered the room and explained to the elderly gentleman what I was about to do. He lifted his hospital gown, and I began to spread out the sterile drape—only to discover that this poor man had no penis, just a stoma, a hole in the pubic arch that led to the bladder. I suppose my dumbfounded expression prompted him to explain: "I lost my little feller to cancer." I expressed genuine sympathy and went on with the successful procedure.

Upon returning to the nurses' station, I was met with bursts of laughter, and a question: "Did you find everything you needed?" I guess nobody has more fun than nurses.

Drunks in an emergency room are a nightly occurrence, sometimes more than three or four on any given Friday or Saturday. Once I was called in during the wee hours to administer a straight catheter to relieve the bladder of a 22-year-old male who had been injured in a drunken bar fight. The fight and the alcohol were still very much in him when I arrived at his cubicle, catheter pack in hand. When he learned what I was about to do, he shouted his objections.

The hospital security guard and I held the inebriated patient fast to the cart, while the attending physician and the nurses attached restraints to his arms and legs. Once he was properly secured, I opened his gown, laid out the sterile drape and luckily was able to hit a moving target as he thrashed about in protest while being relieved of his beer-soaked urine.

I once catheterized an elderly patient and only five minutes later heard a "code blue" announcement over the hospital public address system, which means personnel and a crash cart of lifesaving equipment are immediately dispatched—in this case, to the very same room I had just left. I arrived to see the nurses feverishly working on the gentleman, to no avail. Frantic, I wondered aloud if I had somehow killed him, but was reassured that he was actually brought to the hospital to die, and the catheterization had been ordered to give him some final comfort and relief.

On another occasion I arrived at the room of a 35-year-old patient to shave him before his circumcision procedure. I moved the gown away from his genitalia, created the sterile field, lathered the pubic hair and readied the razor. In shaving the pubic region, the penis has to be moved out of the way with a gloved hand, and shaving is accomplished with the free hand.

Unfortunately, during the process, this guy became aroused, certainly not by me, but from being handled. Mortified, he stammered, "So, uh, how are the, uh, Cincinnati Reds doing?" I was embarrassed for both of us. To make matters worse, this man's wife was a former classmate. Every time I see her, even today, however, she tells me that her ex-husband still laughs about the incident.

I was summoned to an anteroom of the surgery floor early one morning to prep a very large man soon to undergo a cyst removal from his rectum. This enormous person resembled a beached whale as he lay face down on the gurney with his naked behind exposed. I placed the sterile field, liberally lathered the area, and made several attempts to shave his rectum and surrounding tissues. On normal-sized people you can use one hand to push the butt cheeks apart and the other to shave; however, this gentleman's rear end was so huge that I simply could not hold his cheeks apart with one hand. I tried using my left forearm, but there was just too much fat. I walked over to the jovial and resourceful head surgical nurse and described my dilemma. She strolled back to the waiting gentleman, surveyed the situation, reached into the pocket of her white smock and produced a roll of three-inch-wide white surgical tape.

She then instructed me to use both hands and spread the right cheek open as far as I could and attached one end of the tape with the other end lashed to the rail of the gurney. The same procedure was utilized for the left cheek. To my astonishment, the gentleman's butt cheeks were spread so wide you could have parked a bicycle between them. The nurse winked and declared, "That's how you resolve that, honey!"

The hospital setting also provided me with invaluable experience in observing grief. Expressions of grief in a funeral home setting are somewhat toned down in comparison, since friends and relatives are coming to a place where death is already expected. Seeing everyone gathered around a casket to say goodbye is a vision of resolution.

But observing family members congregating in an emergency waiting room, pacing, cursing, sobbing and waiting in terror for a doctor or nurse to arrive with an update, only to be devastated by the worst, most mind-numbing news imaginable, is to watch grief at its full volume.

I have witnessed this scenario many, many times. The ER nurse pokes his or her head into the reception area and then summons the family into a smaller room to await the physician on duty. The doctor arrives and quietly explains that every possible treatment was attempted, to no avail. Reactions range from mere down-turned heads and expressions of resignation to unbridled screams and outbursts of disbelief. It is always torturous.

Ironically, I learned many years ago that allowing family members to view the recently deceased in an emergency room setting can be the embalmer's "friend." In tragic and violent cases where someone is bloody or disfigured, that initial viewing often shocks people into assuming that a closed casket will be their only option. More likely, that bloody corpse is not disfigured at all. Head injuries from auto accidents or gunshots produce a massive amount of blood on the face, but once the blood is cleaned off, only a small laceration or defect is apparent. The face can easily be restored, and the decedent can be viewed in an open casket for a final farewell. Another example of the importance of death "care."

With my career choice firmly in my mind, I was delighted when hospital officials assigned me to morgue duty. The county coroner knew my family and was aware that I was about to enter the Cincinnati College of Mortuary Science, so he was comfortable with my presence in the autopsy room. In those days, Mercy Hospital's morgue was also the official morgue of the Butler County coroner. I soon proved myself as quite proficient at sewing up bodies following hospital-ordered autopsies, so the coroner approached me about doing the same for his own cases. I was more than happy to oblige and was able to witness autopsies in connection with a host of strange and tragic death investigations.

On Easter Sunday, 1975, a crazed 41-year-old man shot and killed his mother, brother, sister-in-law and his brother's eight young children. A surreal scene it was, not only for the number of decedents, but for their manner of death. The children were all shot pointblank with the barrel of the gun obviously pressed right against their heads. Circular black powder burn marks singed the little boys' close-cropped hair, those "buzz-cuts" typical of the era and no doubt received for the upcoming summer. In a room that reeked of formalin and one which usually echoed with friendly and sometimes off-color banter, there were few words exchanged in the midst of such a horrific tragedy.

Most caregivers, whether medical or law enforcement, are reduced to silence and even tears when helpless children are placed upon the autopsy table. As a future funeral director, I was appalled to learn that shortly after these deaths, some local directors were actually quarreling among themselves over how many of the victims they were going to "get."

Yet the autopsy room proved overall to be a great training ground and cemented the fact that death care was definitely the career for me. Although the untimely demise of a child still brings a lump to my throat, the majority of cases I observed were not children. Auto accidents were the most common coroner's cases, and in most instances, autopsies were not performed. The body could be visually examined, and blood would be drawn to determine if alcohol or any other impairment might be present. Gunshot cases, self-inflicted or not, were always fascinating, not only because I could observe the investigation process, but to watch the show put on by the coroner.

A portable x-ray machine would be brought to the morgue, and the coroner was known to insert his ungloved finger into the bullet holes as x-rays were taken to serve as a rudimentary "pointer" that would show up on film. One bank robbery suspect who encountered the police on his way out was hit with two blasts from their shotguns. As he lay on the autopsy table, I removed his clothing and then waited for the coroner and pathologist to begin their work. Then I examined the victim's chest and abdomen wounds. Not only was blood present, but to my amazement what appeared to be fecal matter was oozing out of the holes. The shotgun blasts had apparently pierced not only his lungs and liver, but also several feet of intestines.

When the pathologist arrived my first question was, "Is that crap coming out of those holes?"

His answer was concise and to the point: "Well, you know what they say, Bob. We really are all full of shit."

⤙ S E V E N ⤚

"They Sure Do Good Work Here."

Decapitation, restoration, presentation, suicide—
and the occasional posthumous bust enlargement •

How do you snag the instant attention of a young class of mortuary students—or of anyone else, for that matter? Just mention decapitation. Amazingly enough, it's a far more common cause of death than people think, particularly in cases of industrial or auto accidents.

Back in the 1970s, my classmates and I listened attentively as our embalming instructor detailed the proper procedure for restoring a victim who had suffered the separation of head from body. He outlined for us the fine art of plunging a wooden mop handle, sharpened on both ends, down the spinal column and then positioning the head back onto the shoulders by inserting the

---

• CAUTION: Graphic contents may be disturbing.

opposite end into the corresponding column section. Surrounding skin would then be sutured and the sutures waxed over.

In my 30-plus years as a licensed embalmer, I have utilized this technique on only two occasions. Both victims, one male and one female, were passengers in the same automobile which was struck head-on by a fully loaded gravel truck. Apparently the leading edge of the car's interior windshield frame behaved like a crude guillotine, slicing off the heads of both occupants. Also, due to the tremendous force of the truck, the traumatic injuries incurred were not cleanly administered. Jagged steel and glass slammed into soft flesh, nearly obliterating all facial features. The only way to distinguish which head belonged to which body, in fact, was the obvious long hair with feminine barrettes still affixed. The heads were situated as prescribed back onto the corresponding shoulders, but otherwise there was far too much damage to complete a satisfactory restoration.

"They sure do good work here" is a comment which I have been hearing more and more since I opened my own funeral home in 2001. My wife, who also works with me, did not quite understand its meaning at first. Perhaps she assumed that we were being congratulated on our dignified, compassionate manner and the general care we always provided to client families and our visiting public. But actually, "good work" is the term used in my part of the country to describe how natural dead bodies look while reposing in their respective caskets.

Years ago I worked at a funeral home where comments concerning deceased appearances were universally negative. Rarely were congratulations expressed—much to the ongoing chagrin of my former employer. As the low man on the totem pole and as an infrequent, inexperienced embalmer, my input was neither encouraged nor welcomed. But when the chief embalmer resigned, his duties then fell to me, and a marked improvement began.

My older brother had always stressed that people come to a funeral home to see a deceased loved one looking natural and well-groomed. The smallest details, from buffed fingernails and hand placement to an impeccable knot in a gentleman's necktie are all equally essential. That dedication to a dignified presentation has stuck with me to this day, and I have repeatedly stressed and ranted to my own sons that such devotion to duty is the only option that I will accept.

In time, my former boss, who no longer felt the need to enter the preparation room at all, was duly impressed and delighted with the satisfaction suddenly enjoyed by his clientele. In those archaic times he would greet the deceased's family upon their arrival and then take full credit for the "good work" as if he himself had performed every prepping stage.

My next stop on the employment road found me at a funeral home where the employees felt as I did—that the attractive appearance of the deceased, not the sale of an expensive casket, should be the ultimate goal. Although most funeral home visitors may briefly admire the casket in which the decedent is reposing, with a spray of flowers adorning it and other bouquets blanketing the entire chapel area, it can be difficult to distinguish one from another. The deceased loved one is the star. Rarely have I heard departing guests whisper, "Wow, Stan sure had a beautiful casket." More likely it's, "Wow, Stan looked like he could get up and talk to you; they sure do good work here."

That good work unfortunately seems to be missing from today's corporately owned funeral homes. The company's stock exchange performance and the general manager's bonus expectations are of far more importance. One result is the purging of experienced embalmers and funeral directors in favor of kids fresh out of mortuary school who lack the proper seasoning but whose salary requirements meet bottom-line qualifications. As an elderly embalmer informed me many years ago, "It takes at least ten years to become a professional." I share that adage with my sons on a daily basis.

To present a dead human for viewing to his or her grieving family sounds like a strange custom. Why is it necessary that the deceased be present for funeralization to take place? Simple. It satisfies the need to say goodbye to a vessel which once held a beloved soul and therefore still carries a strong emotional attachment.

In *The American Way of Death (1963)*, author Jessica Mitford heavily criticized the way that we Americans care for our dead, particularly in regard to our purchases of ornate and costly caskets. Ms. Mitford also railed about the funeral ceremony itself and the display of a dead individual looking as if alive. Her scathing book gained a substantial following and was moving quickly toward universal acceptance—until a sudden, tragic pivotal event occurred. President John F. Kennedy was assassinated mere months after her book's release.

What did America see for the first time on live national television? A funeral of the grandest proportions, complete with a dead human contained in a very expensive solid mahogany casket. This casket, by the way, was provided by a funeral home in Washington, D.C. Upon Kennedy's death on November 22, the Secret Service contacted a Dallas funeral home to come to Parkland Memorial Hospital with the finest casket available. The dutiful director arrived with a 48-ounce solid bronze casket into which Kennedy's unembalmed body was placed. The President was then spirited off to the airport and flown to Andres Air Force Base for an autopsy by Naval doctors.

It was later reported that an actual tug-of-war with President Kennedy's body occurred between Secret Service agents and the Dallas county sheriff. The high sheriff correctly noted that a homicide victim should be autopsied in the county of death, but he was overruled, and the body left Dallas encased in solid bronze. The temporary casket was never paid for, although the Dallas funeral director billed the Kennedy family on numerous occasions. It is said that he caused so much furor over the unpaid bill that his business suffered greatly and eventually closed. That same bronze casket was stored in the basement of the White House for several years until 1967, when Robert F. Kennedy, the President's brother, had it unceremoniously dropped into the Atlantic Ocean.

Secret Service agents accompanied Kennedy's body throughout its travels, from the trip back to Washington, D.C, to the Naval Hospital autopsy room and finally to the funeral home in Washington. One agent, unimpressed with the pomp and circumstance of funeralization and believing the embalming process was a crude, barbaric and unnecessary procedure, queried that since there was so much damage to Kennedy's head, why not just cremate him? Later, however, that same agent was reported to have been totally amazed at the work of the embalmers and their restoration process. He had watched as the formaldehyde-based chemical was injected and the color quickly came back into the President's face. The Kennedy family was able to privately view the body in a most presentable state, looking very natural—unlike what Mrs. Kennedy had experienced in Dallas, when she was photographed attempting to retrieve pieces of her husband's skull and brain tissue from the trunk lid of their open limousine.

So the question remains: Is it really a good thing to embalm and restore a body, then cosmetize and dress it in its Sunday best to be displayed as if alive? Ironically, in nearly every case, the family is very satisfied with the cosmetized appearance of the deceased when that person is over 75 years of age. Things happen the way they're supposed to--we live a long, good life, and then we die. An elderly person is better off, we believe, not suffering or becoming a burden.

A young person, on the other hand, presents not only the ultimate grief experience to his or her family, but is too often compounded by a need, since young people tend to die tragically, for extensive restoration. A face that has been bludgeoned, smashed, traumatized, burned, lacerated or exposed to the ravages of cancer presents a challenge too, regardless of how sharp the funeral director's skills may be. There is no greater sense of helplessness than needing to tell a mother and father that their son or daughter cannot be viewed due to too much disease or damage, not enough body parts, too many days in the July sun or too many weeks of lying in a river.

Summer heat results in a body that has turned on itself. Stomach acids and gases erode and destroy the vessel from the inside out. Once maggots develop, that body can be reduced to a skeleton in a matter of days. Too much time submerged in deep water creates similar decomposition problems with a greater incidence of bloating and discoloration, often resulting in a closed casket.

If any semblance of a face is still present, however, then restoration can still take place. Even blunt force trauma in an auto accident is usually repaired with time-tested methods. Lacerations are secured with super-glue, rather than sewn, which leaves a raised trail from the thread. Broken facial bones are pushed back into place and wired together. Large holes from rearview mirrors, radio knobs, gear shift levers, turn-signal stalks and windshield glass can be filled with wax and reshaped like the former contours of the face. Lips, orbital bones and even eyeballs can be fashioned from wax. Eyebrows, eyelashes and facial hair can be harvested from the back of the deceased's head and then inserted into soft wax in the appropriate areas.

However, a body run over by a train, caught in an explosion, hit by a shotgun blast, killed in a plane crash or burned in a fire is generally a hopeless case. BBR, or burned beyond recognition, is a lost cause; there is only a black skeleton to work with. I have attempted such a facial reconstruction with poor results. Working from a recent photo, I have constructed a face and all of its features from wax, filled clothing with cotton to simulate chest, arms and abdomen and even attached white gloves to the cuffs of a blouse so that hands appeared present. Not a very natural appearance, but close enough for a family to derive some sort of closure from a devastating loss.

Once I discovered the utility of Plaster of Paris, restoring large defects of the head became simpler. A young man I cared for recently was attempting to discover what object was obstructing the travel of a large hydraulic press at an automotive parts production facility. He placed his head inside it, and unfortunately, the press engaged and flattened his head to the shape of a pancake.

After embalming the lower portion of the body, I set out to repair his head. The press had caused massive scalp and facial tears, so I knew there would be a great deal of super glue involved. I used my gloved hand to push wet Plaster of Paris into the area that was once his mouth, and amazingly enough, the plaster expanded as it dried. I continued to push the material into the defect until it completely popped his features back into an almost normal position. I was then able to glue the multiple lacerations and apply cosmetics to eventually achieve a very natural appearance.

During summer months, there are not only increased cases of rapid decomposition due to drownings, but also cases where a person happens to die alone at home and is not discovered for several days. With severe decomposition, the skin slips off the body, bloating occurs, and the tremendously offensive odor does not allow normal viewing. In years past, a formaldehyde-based chemical was poured over it to mask the odor, but even that could not completely eliminate the smell.

So a funeral director employer of mine from many years ago introduced me to the positive effects of agricultural lime. Lime is the white drying agent familiar to those who watch Mafia-themed movies, where hit men bury dispatched victims in shallow graves and then cover the bodies with fifty or one hundred pounds of lime. Because it rapidly absorbs any liquids, in the case of a decomposing human body, those odiferous liquids are eliminated; thus the body is less likely to be discovered. In this day and age, however, skeletal remains can still be identified.

As a farmer, this man had poured lime into the graves of dead livestock and rightly assumed the same treatment would suffice for humans. Whether the deceased is placed in a normal closed casket or in a cremation container, a bed of lime eight inches deep is poured in first, and then the entire body is covered. This process requires two fifty-pound bags, but within minutes the odor is eliminated. I have also used lime on decubitus ulcers (bedsores) and other odor problems with wonderful results. Other funeral directors in my area have called to inquire about how to handle agricultural lime in a funeral home setting.

The value of embalming, on the other hand, is ultimately in the eye of the beholder. Is it a good thing that embalming permits the dead human body to decompose more cleanly? It has been written many times that the Egyptians were the first true embalmers. I would have to agree. Even Biblical accounts report that the dead Jesus was anointed with spices, no doubt to abate inevitable odors. The Egyptians removed the brain through the nostrils with a pointed tool and then inserted natron-soaked linens. The abdominal organs were also removed, and that area was treated as well. Those organs carried a mystical value and were stored in decorative jars with carved lids depicting certain animals. The body was then wrapped in linen sheets dipped in some sort of spice or preservative—and *voila!* A mummy.

This crude embalming process, however, was only partially successful. The arid Egyptian climate lacked humidity, a weather condition which speeds decomposition. Without humidity the body simply dries up if left outdoors, whether any preservation is attempted or not. Today the embalming process buys time— enough time to hold a funeral visitation and service three or four days following a death.

Many years ago I embalmed the body of a 22-year old man who was hit by a passing freight train. Luckily he was killed instantaneously upon impact. But the engine did not pass over his body; he was flung alongside the tracks. Since this occurred back in the 1970s, long before the days of obligatory lawsuits, an autopsy was not performed. The county coroner correctly determined at the scene that this was an obvious accidental death.

But since this man carried no identification, I embalmed the body and then held it. Three weeks went by, with several visits from grieving parents of missing sons, all deeply torn. Their pain was excruciating to watch. Might we now bury our long-lost boy and perhaps derive some sort of closure? Or do we pray that this body is not really his?

"Formaldehyde gray" was meanwhile making its presence known; however, facial features were still clearly recognizable. A massage cream had been liberally applied to retain pliability of tissues, and I soon decided to add paste cosmetics to mask the impending changes.

Identification finally came five weeks later. A trembling father had seen flyers published in his local newspaper. His son had stormed out after a disagreement over farm chores. But by that time he was identifiable primarily by his unique work boots—and a missing ring finger from an earlier tractor accident on his dad's property.

I once removed the body of a young man from underneath a school bus he had been repairing. The jacks supporting the bus had failed, and he was unfortunately crushed by the rear dual wheels. The other unfortunate part was that he was working alone during the noon hour when other mechanics had left for lunch. When his coworkers returned, they made a horrific discovery.

This man had already been underneath the bus for at least an hour, and another hour or so passed before my arrival—ample time for nature's effects, such as the gathering of flies. I brought him back to the funeral home to begin the embalming process and noticed some tiny fly larvae in the corner of his mouth and the corner of one eye. I brushed them aside and thought nothing more of it.

After meeting with the young man's mother the next day to make the funeral arrangements, she requested viewing her son immediately, even before he was dressed and placed in his casket. I asked her to join me back at the funeral home in two hours. Thank goodness I granted myself the extra time.

When I went into the preparation room, I was aghast. When I looked at the man's face, it appeared to be moving. With a pair of tweezers I pulled open his mouth and found it full of slimy, squirming maggots. I dipped cotton into liquid formaldehyde and pushed it inside, but it had little effect on those rascals, and being a novice in the funeral business at that time, I was at a loss as to my next move. I called my more experienced older brother. He sagely informed me that since maggots have a slimy coating, only kerosene would kill them. So that's what I used.

On a much happier restorative note, many embalmers routinely fill women's brassieres with cotton afterward to duplicate the appearance of full, lifelike breasts. But the proper quantity sometimes involves a bit of guesswork. One grieving husband confronted me upon first viewing his late wife in her casket, inquiring as to how I had magically increased her bust size. At first I was apprehensive, thinking he might be angry with me—but then he winked and told me his wife would be proud to be sporting such an exquisite pair.

Suicides present their own unique restorative challenges. My first experience came as a wide-eyed 15-year-old. My brother and I were dispatched to a residence to remove the victim of a self-inflicted shotgun blast to the face. It was considered in its day a simple, open-and-shut case. The coroner had already come and gone and granted permission for the deceased to be removed. The man's daughter greeted us at the front door and showed us into a small first-floor bathroom with just a commode, a sink—and a ceiling literally coated with fragments of human tissue.

The man had placed the shotgun in his mouth as he sat on the toilet seat. His head was nearly gone; the blast had blown away all structures from the upper lip and above. Brain and skull pieces with hair still attached adorned the ceiling and hung downward like stalactites. Only the lower jaw still rested upon the decedent's neck.

I was so stunned that I barely remember the removal procedure. Did we carry in the litter or just roll up the cot to the bathroom door? Who knows?

The daughter followed us outside to the hearse and asked if part of our job was to scrub down the bathroom. My brother said no. However, when the woman said she would pay someone "a handsome sum" to do so, I readily spoke up. But my brother nixed the deal, saying that if I did a poor job, her family might not ever call our establishment again. Just as well, since I don't know how I would have tackled that mess—although my 15-year-old mind kept spinning endlessly in regard to what "a handsome sum" might be.

Several years ago a wealthy gentleman used two different methods to try to end his own life. I knew him as a successful entrepreneur with all of the proper high-society trappings. His wife was having a clandestine love affair, a fact well-known throughout the community. When the husband found out, though, he chose immediately to end his pain.

He was found in his garaged silver Porsche 914 with a single gunshot wound to the right temple. Also discovered at the scene was a garden hose threaded into the driver's side window, with the opposite end attached to the chrome-tipped exhaust pipe. The carbon monoxide ingestion attempt obviously did not bring death soon enough, so the Charter Arms .32 pistol became his more successful Plan B.

How convenient for the wife. Hubby was now out of the picture, and she had a new man with whom to share her money.

Yet when she spoke at her husband's funeral, she delivered a stirring eulogy complimenting her late husband's drive and determination. "Whether it was in making money or in the way he ended his life," she stated without a trace of irony, "whatever he set his mind to do, he did it with determination." The deceased man's parents were no doubt dismayed at their daughter-in-law's positive spin.

The Jeremiah Morrow Bridge spanning the Little Miami River is thought to be the highest bridge in the state of Ohio. That fact alone probably makes it a popular leaping platform. On four separate occasions I have removed bodies from beneath that span—all males. In each case the leaper did not land directly below or in the water. Each slammed about halfway up the deep V-shaped crevasse that develops naturally beneath a bridge.

In two cases which occurred in the spring—the muddy time of year—the bodies were almost totally concealed in the earth. When I arrived on the scene, in fact, they had to be literally pointed out to me, since there was no evidence whatsoever from a distance. The bridge's height coupled with the body's weight drove each decedent into the soft ground, in each case with the victim's shoes barely peeking out.

A recently widowed 65-year-old woman, quite the stylish dresser, decided to end her life in an elegant and dramatic way. She had dressed herself in new underclothes, silk pajamas and a very expensive antique bed jacket. Her surviving daughter showed me the letter her mother had left behind, detailing why her life had to end—and leaving specific instructions for me: "Make sure Mr. Webster carefully removes my present clothing, does what he needs to do to my body for preparation, and then places those same clothes on me for my funeral." Her bedroom, now a death chamber, was festooned with scented candles and vases filled with flowers. The woman had ingested 75 Sominex sleeping tablets and then washed them down with a half bottle of champagne.

But her last meal had been Mexican pizza, which disagreed with her other ingestions, and the combined mixture spoiled her notion of a dignified death in a beautiful setting. She was found, not peacefully reposing on her four-poster bed, hands folded across her chest, clad in her personally selected finery—but curled up on the bathroom floor, her facial features wracked from hours of violent vomiting and unforgiving bowels. The beautiful nightclothes she'd chosen for her funeral were soiled and foul. They were unceremoniously disposed of by her daughter, and a more mundane outfit was quickly provided.

Suicide is never a neat or easy remedy for resolving life's challenges. It's always messy—and horrifying to those who are forced to view the aftereffects. Think about it. The person who ultimately endures the shock of discovering your body is too often the one whom you love most.

"Mom's Favorite Grandchild, Freddy..."

Caskets versus coffins, the "leakage" factor, vaults and mausoleums, cremation, disinterment—and the thorny business of composing a proper obituary

The stately steel or wooden container in which we place a deceased loved one is still the focal point of any funeral. Although grief therapists adamantly insist that a funeral is for the living, attendees are generally presented with a chapel setting which features the deceased—the person to be respected, honored and viewed. In most cases, he or she is nattily attired and posed as if sleeping in a bed-like box designed to look attractive and comfortable.

This box can be constructed of the most spartan materials or of the most expensive metals—and everywhere in between. Just like cars, caskets are offered as basic squares with few frills, and then may become elaborately crafted units with velvet interiors and leather-wrapped carrying handles.

The cheapest caskets are made of thick cardboard and covered with doeskin cloth. Their interiors are fitted with low-grade crepe and correspondingly inexpensive pillows. Such lightweights are used for both in-ground burials and pre-cremation viewings. Some funeral homes also use them for indigent decedents when little or no payment is expected.

Cloth-covered wood is the next step upward, with particle board covered in blue, gray or burgundy-embossed cloth. Interiors are also inexpensive, sometimes with a filler of wood shavings in lieu of bedding. Still featured in funeral homes' display rooms, they serve a useful purpose, either by being readily burnable when visitations are followed by cremation—or by looking so cheap that families turn away in horror and instantly upgrade to more expensive models.

The next category of caskets is 20-gauge steel. Gauges range from 20, the thinnest, to 18 or 16, the thickest and therefore the most expensive. Caskets of 20-gauge are virtually all shaped the same, but are available in a variety of exterior and interior colors. As prices rise, trim options increase as well—two-tone color schemes, better interior materials and even swing bar handles on the outside.

The most basic, bottom-of-the-heap 20-gauge is a non-sealer, where the lid has a small metal catch that attaches to a corresponding hole in the front when closed. A 20-gauge sealer casket features a seamless rubber gasket attached to the upper portion of the box. When the lid is closed, a crank is inserted into a hole at the right front (foot end) of the casket and cranked closed via a gear system that forces the lid onto the rubber gasket, thus supposedly rendering the casket permanently closed.

I have often questioned whether an actual seal is accomplished by using this system, as has the Federal Trade Commission, which now instructs funeral directors to inform families that a sealer casket equipped with a rubber gasket is resistant to air and water. Congratulating a family on such a wise move enabled funeral directors of the past to reassure folks that their deceased loved one would remain in a state of suspended animation rather than succumb to the forces of decomposition. I suspect that claim has no merit. At far too many mausoleums in mid-July I've experienced the pungent bouquet emanating from those supposed sealers.

The next level is 18-gauge steel. This middle-of-the-road option is the most popular choice among the casket-buying public and what the National Funeral Directors Association refers to as an average sale. Most grieving families do not want to appear cheap, and this medium-priced model fills the bill nicely. I have probably heard it a thousand times: "We don't want the best, but we don't want the cheapest, either. Show us something priced in the middle."

Virtually every color (and combination of colors) is available, as well as interior upgrades, such as velvets, tailoring and head cap panels, custom-designed with any theme imaginable. Prices range from $900 to $4000. Funeral homes generally employ a 1.5x markup to arrive at that retail figure—but I've heard tales of homes charging four or even five times their wholesale price. The majority of homes nationwide offer 18-gauge steel caskets at reasonable and affordable prices, and such caskets have thus become the benchmarks of successful sales.

Stainless steel caskets are the next step upward, and the obvious quality and eye appeal more than justify the price increase. Brushed tops add a sophisticated finish. Aurora Casket Company used to market stainless steel caskets to housewives, hoping they would recall their gleaming kitchen appliances. Placards propped in selected caskets even featured an attractive, apron-clad woman smiling as she admired her clean stainless steel sink.

A solid copper casket has been the Holy Grail for funeral directors since the 1950s. I recall as a 15-year-old hearing tales of that elusive but finally consummated copper sale. The successful funeral director would be beside himself with pride, relating to his wide-eyed peers just how he'd accomplished his feat: "They were looking real hard at the 18-gauge bronzetone, but then they turned around and told me they liked the copper, because it would never rust!"

My supervisor many years ago was a classy, white-haired gentleman, a sharp dresser and a genuinely nice person. He sold more copper caskets in a single year than anyone I have ever known, and when he did, he would announce, "I sold a copper....again." That pause before "again" was probably a motivational tool to encourage us peons to hawk something better than 18-gauges.

This same supervisor, held in such awesome esteem by his employees, had a habit of making us feel uncomfortable when we did in fact accomplish a respectable copper-or-better sale. He was rightly concerned about where the payment was coming from, particularly with a high-end product. On many occasions I had to explain in detail exactly who was paying the bill, whether insurance proceeds were involved, and most importantly, how soon the payment could be expected. It was always satisfying when I was able to stroll into his office, report the good news of a high-powered casket sale and then hand him the signed contract, complete with an envelope full of cash stapled to it—in other words, a paid-in-full account. My coworkers were sometimes envious of my ability to convince families to pay by the very day of the service; however, in most cases, I was merely lucky that I had met with people wishing to get it all over with.

Caskets made of solid bronze are the costliest and probably the most impressive-looking of all. Bronze sales are rare, and when they occur, most funeral directors are beside themselves with glee. Obviously, as the wholesale cost increases, so does the retail markup and profit margin. Entry-level bronze caskets retail for nearly $5,000 for a low-end and up to $9,000 for a high-end. A gold-plated, solid bronze casket that wholesales for $17,000 would sell in some markets for $34,000.

Whenever I travel I make a point to secure a general and casket price list from a funeral home or two. During a recent trip to Los Angeles, I discovered that at one home, charging three times wholesale was common practice. I realize the cost of living is higher there than in Ohio, but that was blatantly ridiculous.

When I first began my career in the funeral business, solid bronzes were referred to as gangster caskets. From reading about the Mafia and seeing the mobster movies of the day, I learned that a great send off seemed to be part of their public image. One of the first embalming fluid salesmen I met was based in Chicago. I always looked forward to his calls because of his spellbinding tales regarding his father's funeral home on the south side of Chicago in the late 1920s and early 1930s. The father had been approached by a ranking Mafia member and informed that his business had become the local syndicate's funeral home of choice. When he was handed $10,000 in cash to seal the relationship, this gentleman realized they were totally serious. He had better play ball.

Supposedly, his first job for the Mafia was to place a bullet-riddled body beneath the bed of a casket already occupied by a recently deceased person. The funeral took place with two occupants, one hidden, in the same casket. This act was repeated several times over the years, with a few complaints from pallbearers who were probably amazed at the heavy weight they were carrying.

When the practice became riskier than our Chicago director had wished, the Mafia partners supposedly equipped his establishment with the South Side's first crematorium. Cremating dispatched enemies was so much easier, with far less evidence left behind, so a whole new cottage industry developed. The funeral director was said to still receive his standard fee for services rendered.

Although mobsters often kill among their own numbers, most are traditionalists when it comes to funeralization, and they generally insist on a Catholic Mass. To cremate an enemy and obliterate the body, as described by my Chicago acquaintance, indicated a total lack of respect.

Copper and bronze do not rust. Casket companies have emphasized that point in their promotional materials in hopes that intelligent and progressive funeral directors will impart such information to families—and push the belief that if such a unit would remain pristine over many years in the grave, then the human body contained therein would also remain so. Casket companies used to provide funeral directors with small copper and bronze samples to display inside caskets so that consumers could touch them and imagine how genuinely protected their deceased loved ones would be. The Statue of Liberty, also constructed of copper, was a popular lithograph displayed in caskets to tout copper's durability, as were photos of copper gutters on expensive homes.

I once drove to a funeral home in Kentucky to bring back an accident victim and was given The Grand Tour of the small town's establishment. In his office the owner proudly showed me several framed awards proclaiming his home as the top seller of copper and bronze caskets for many years in a row. His casket supplier was no doubt equally excited. What I found most intriguing was that every casket in his display room was either solid copper or solid bronze! No wonder he sold so many. I asked him what happened when a family of modest means came to him for service. He responded that everyone in his area knew that when they patronized him, they'd better bring along plenty of money.

The average retail bronze casket is priced at $8500, so it is not a very common purchase. The few times, perhaps twice a year, that I have sold a solid bronze, it is almost an unbelievable experience—although in my own mind, it's difficult to justify such an expenditure by a consumer who is only going to enjoy his purchase for a few days.

In my experience most bronze sales are not to the ultra-rich, but to the middle class. The first time I ever sold a solid bronze was to a retired General Motors factory worker who had saved money over the years specifically earmarked for his wife's burial. He didn't trust life insurance salesmen and even opted not to accept the insurance offered by GM through payroll deduction. Still, he told me he wanted the most expensive casket for his beloved spouse, and he didn't care what it cost.

When I informed him that his expenses would total $6150 (a hefty funeral bill in 1977), he asked me to come to his home to collect. As we sat at his kitchen table, I learned that this gentleman also had no use for banks. I watched in amazement as he pulled hundred dollar bills, one by one, all rolled tightly, out of an entire row of old olive jars.

Each time he reached a thousand dollars, he asked me to re-roll the bills in the opposite direction so they could be smoothed out to be counted. Our transaction complete, I went straight to the bank to deposit the money that still reeked of olives, as did my fingers. He had apparently never thought to rinse out the jars.

Expensive caskets, such as 16-gauge steel, stainless steel, solid copper and solid bronze, are sometimes urn-shaped rather than rectangular. This urn shape is not only more attractive and costlier, it also serves a practical purpose for funeral directors. The extra inch or so of additional width inside allows us to position a heavier person in a more comfortable repose. With arms crossed across the abdomen, the elbows rest against the interior sides of the casket. If the deceased is overweight, a little extra elbow room is sometimes just enough to position the arms and hands into a normal state. Without the extra room, the deceased appears, and is, stuffed uncomfortably into the casket.

For obese decedents, 350 pounds and up, oversize caskets must be utilized. A normal casket's interior dimensions are 23 inches wide and 78 inches long. Oversize caskets are available in widths of 27, 30 and 34 inches. For the morbidly obese, custom-made caskets must be specially manufactured and are usually available in two or three days.

A high-end casket, along with many mid-priced ones, is always equipped with a plastic tray positioned strategically underneath the dead body. It's known as a fail-safe liner. Embalming and other fluids frequently ooze from the deceased even if an expert and thorough embalming job has taken place. Incisions that are improperly dried or not stitched tightly enough have also been known to leak, as well as the site of the trocar, where we embalmers insert a thin, tube-like instrument just above the belly button to aspirate the thoracic and abdominal cavities.

An obese decedent presents an additional problem due to the immense pressure on the abdomen caused by sheer girth and also the weight of arms and hands resting on the belly. Many years ago I was approached at a visitation by the deceased's spouse. Her husband was morbidly obese. She asked me to explain the appearance of moisture and an odd sound emanating as he reposed in his casket. Luckily he was dressed in a black sport shirt which hid the wetness—however, as I held my ear to his huge belly, I could distinguish a bass-like sound similar to the opening notes of the 1960s gag song, "Tie Me Kangaroo Down Sport." I asked those gathered to leave the room for a moment while I investigated further.

I pulled up his shirt and undershirt and discovered that the trocar hole, originally closed with a threaded plastic button, was belching liquid, probably propelled by a belly full of gas. His immense girth and the pressure of arms and hands had forced this gaseous liquid outward and onto his clothing.

I replaced the trocar button, laid plastic sheeting against his bare belly and then sprayed Lysol around the casket. It sufficed until the visitation was over, and later we were able to treat the problem more thoroughly. I had not been the embalmer in this case; whoever was had obviously not treated the thoracic and abdominal organs properly.

A burial vault is the box-shaped concrete receptacle into which a casket is placed. Such grave liners originated many years ago after some unpleasant incidents following the burials of a few wealthy early Americans. Rich people were known to bury their women in not only their finest clothing, but also with precious jewels. The gravedigger, perhaps a private contractor or even the undertaker himself, would return to the cemetery under the cover of darkness, dig up the fresh grave, open the casket just wide enough to get a hand inside and then remove the fancy jewelry and sometimes even gold-filled teeth!

A rich industrialist from Pennsylvania had heard of such atrocious acts, and upon the death of his beloved wife, he instructed a crew of employees to assemble wrought iron fencing inside her open grave. Her casket was to be lowered into the protective cage, a wrought iron lid placed on top and then covered with dirt. At the time this was thought to be quite the innovation. Later, however, the gravedigger could still insert his hands between the iron bars, gain access to the casket and still ably remove the contents. To prevent robbery, the casket needed to be completely encapsulated.

Eventually, bedecking deceased loved ones in expensive jewelry went out of style, so crude wooden grave boxes were still considered acceptable liners. But as cemeteries began to fill up with more and more decedents, Mother Nature taught us that wood did not hold up well underground. Changes in weather, insect activity and, of course, moisture caused many a box to decompose, thus causing the grave to partially cave in. Cemetery operators found that they were spending many hours refilling those graves and even resorted to planting English ivy or myrtle on top to help hide disappearing earth.

The arrival of concrete ushered in the notion of a manufactured burial vault. Concrete was solid enough to prove an ideal barrier against moisture and other elements. Also, the dirt used to fill an adult grave is of tremendous weight, and with vehicles and other cemetery machinery traveling overhead, a stout burial vault not only keeps it from collapsing, but also protects the casket and its precious resident.

A concrete box is just what it sounds like—a large grave liner with a lid; however, it possesses no sealing properties. The lid is merely placed on top, where it fits flush with the leading edge of the bottom portion. It is, therefore, not a vault. A vault is constructed with reinforced steel rods for added strength, much like a sidewalk. It also carries some degree of protection, since it is constructed tongue-in-groove and equipped with a thick, tar-like sealant. Vault manufacturers have resorted to dressing up their products with such costly amenities as copper, bronze, stainless steel and fiberglass liners, and even lids decorated with religious emblems and pastoral scenes. As with supposed sealed caskets, the FTC requires that funeral homes do not warrant vaults—although manufacturers may choose to do so. Also, due to a lack of training or simple downright deception, some cemeteries are still selling unsuspecting consumers inexpensive, non-protective concrete boxes, all the while referring to them as vaults.

Air-sealed vaults constructed of steel, stainless steel and copper are still utilized today, but to a much lesser degree. The air seal-principle is like turning a water glass upside down in a filled sink. The air pressure inside the glass keeps the water from reaching a certain level, such as the level of a casket in a grave. In an air-sealed vault installation, a flat piece of steel fits level on the bottom of the grave; after the casket is lowered, the casket rests directly on that flat piece. The dome or top of the vault is then lowered into the grave, where the dome snaps into place, thus creating an air-seal principle, which in turn keeps the elements from contacting the casket.

The few times I have used air vaults were connected with burials in remote family cemeteries in the Kentucky and West Virginia hills. There is no way to haul a heavy concrete burial vault up the side of a mountain or down into a steep hollow, so the perfect choice is a steel air-seal. The bottom and top are easily placed in a pickup truck bed, driven to the grave site and then put into place. After the bottom and the casket are positioned, two men can carry the dome to the grave and install it with canvas grave straps. In a less remote location, an air-seal vault is installed with normal machinery and a cable-equipped hoist for lowering the dome.

Elaborate personal mausoleums—once reserved for the very wealthy—are constructed on cemetery grounds and allow for entombment of both husband and wife, sometimes even entire families. Most folks who select mausoleums do not wish to be buried in the ground, and assume that a crypt results in a much cleaner disposition. But since decomposition is accelerated by heat, just imagine the speed when the recently deceased is placed in a steel casket, and that casket is slid into a crypt twenty feet above ground level in midsummer. Even a well-embalmed body will ooze fluids over time, although in a steel sealed casket, it should present no problems whatsoever in a mausoleum setting.

When certain conditions are breeched, however, such as a poorly embalmed or unembalmed body, using a cheap or non-sealing casket such as hardwood, or shortcuts being taken by the embalmer or mausoleum operator, then some horrific and disgusting events can occur. I advocate the use of lime in any casket destined for mausoleum entombment. Pour a three or four-inch inch bed across the entire length and width of the casket's bottom, and any fluids will be totally absorbed. Even sealed steel caskets have small pin holes in the corners, and, of course, liquids follow the path of least resistance. Mausoleum operators should therefore not allow a non-sealing casket of any kind, steel or hardwood, to be placed in a crypt. A few mausoleum operators offer for sale a huge, thick plastic bag that surrounds the casket and is zipped up before crypt placement. A good idea, yet some family members either cannot afford such an option or simply choose not to do so.

I have seen evidence, both indoors and outdoors, of bodily fluids that have leaked out of the crypt and down the wall onto the spaces between a mausoleum's granite letters. Accompanying any leakage is the obvious odor. During the summer months, while conducting funeral services in a mausoleum chapel teeming with that stench, it can become nearly unbearable. Mourners walk through the doors and then look at each other in stunned disbelief, as if to ask, "What's that awful smell?"

Cremation is performed by placing a dead human body in a casket or other combustible container such as a cardboard box and then placing the occupied container in a cremation chamber or retort, where it is subjected to intense heat and flame. Through the use of natural gas burners, incineration of both the container and its human contents is accomplished, and substances are consumed or driven off—except for bone fragments and metal, such as dental gold and silver, medical devices or implants. The remaining non-burnable skeletal fragments are then mechanically processed (pulverized) in what appears to be a huge Waring blender. These processed cremains or ashes are then placed in a temporary plastic container or urn of one's choice for final "disposition"—burial, scattering, placing on the family mantel or in a columbarium niche, a structure designated specifically for the deposit of urns containing cremains. A columbarium is a smaller-scale mausoleum. Natives of India opt for cremation for religious reasons, followed by a pilgrimage to India in order to scatter the ashes into the Ganges River.

The outside appearance of a typical rental casket, often used in cremation cases, is highly polished. A cardboard tray insert, hidden by overlay material, is already positioned in the bed area. After the funeral service, the deceased is slid out of the casket at one end through a drop-down door, a lid is secured on the cardboard insert, and the deceased goes to the crematory. A new interior and cardboard insert are then slid back into the casket for the next occupant.

I have encountered several situations in which a rental casket unit was abhorred. One man desired complete funeralization followed by cremation for his late wife. He absolutely loathed the idea that she would be taken out of the rental and then cremated in a simple cardboard box. He wanted to purchase a very expensive solid cherry casket, hold the funeral service, and then cremate her in the purchased casket. He got his wish.

A gay man requested the same thing, but with a few extraordinary quirks: He insisted on being with the body of his mate throughout the entire death care process. When his friend died, he had followed the hearse from the hospital to the funeral home and had waited just outside the preparation room while embalming took place. Afterward, the decedent was placed on a dressing table, attired in a favorite set of silk pajamas and robe and rolled into the chapel for an initial inspection.

The next day, the man returned, styled his late friend's hair and purchased a stately solid walnut casket. After the service, he followed the hearse to the crematory and even assisted in rolling his friend's casketed body into the crematory receiving area. The operator, realizing he had a grieving person observing his every move, made an exception to his usual routine. Normally he would remove the casket lids, knock down the sides and ends with a sledgehammer, then pile the casket material in a corner to be burned on another day. Taking the casket apart down to only the bed on which the deceased is lying allows for a faster cremation and less fuel usage. But this time the entire casket and its deceased cargo were inserted into the retort, under the watchful eyes of a grieving friend.

Cremation is a growing trend that is ever so slowly making its way into my part of the country, which is still primarily a ground-burial belt. Casket manufacturers are feverishly attempting to assist funeral directors by developing new profit producers associated with cremation products and services. From fancier low-end cremation caskets to more expensive cremation urns, directors in the Midwest are going through a "feeling out" period—trying to determine what consumers will deem valuable, and more importantly, what they'll be willing to pay extra for.

After attending a few casket company-sponsored seminars specifically designed to introduce the newest offerings relative to cremation, I have to admit to being amazed at the possibilities: Cremation-friendly caskets with themed head panels, just like those offered on expensive steel caskets. A myriad of urns from the most basic to the most elaborate. Mini-urns that match normal capacity versions, so that children can be presented with a small amount of their grandmother's ashes. Stainless steel bracelets equipped with small openings in order to deposit a smidgeon of ashes and covered later with screw-on birthstone caps. Even necklaces with mini-urns attached to the chain! I have actually sold many of these products, so perhaps the casket manufacturers are on to something. If they offer it, someone will probably buy it.

I once believed that only wealthy and highly educated people desired cremation. The funeral home where I worked as a teenager was then the firm of choice for the area's upper crust, and I was often puzzled as to why doctors and lawyers were not given full-service funerals with all the trimmings. I was told that these families had selected cremation for generations, because it was simpler and less stressful for the survivors.

I didn't buy it. I believed that it was really because these people didn't have time for a grieving period and also didn't want to spend any unnecessary money. Perhaps the rich and the learned of my area had brought their death care philosophies with them when they'd arrived from other countries two generations earlier. Since Ohio, Kentucky, Indiana and surrounding environs are well-known for favoring ground burials, cremation was a rare selection. The cremation rate nears 60% in the big metropolises of the East and West coasts.

Perhaps those outside of my area feel that viewing the body and other associated rites are barbaric or the actions of dullards and others beneath them in terms of economic and educational status. I have noticed that if an economically challenged family with Southern roots is offered cremation when funds are lacking, the response is disdain or even anger. Working-class people used to consider the idea of cremation an affront. Today it's a more acceptable option, though still not nearly as popular as casketed ground burial. One contributing factor is its growing acceptance by Roman Catholics, who previously deemed cremation as taboo.

Also adding to the increase is the higher cost of funerals and especially cemetery charges. Grave space prices, charges for opening/closing graves and burial vault requirements have increased disproportionately compared to other rate-of-inflation spikes. When a single grave space costs a family $1500, opening and closing it costs $900, and a required vault costs $800, then that family has to come up with $3200 before even speaking with a funeral director. Opting for cremation eliminates that charge.

Cremation-related services can be separated into three distinct categories. First, immediate cremation or direct cremation—the body is cremated shortly after death, with no accompanying ceremonies or rites. The body is removed, placed in a minimum (cardboard) container, and after an arrangement conference with the decedent's family and acquiring proper signatures, the containerized decedent is cremated, with the ashes delivered in either a spartan plastic temporary container or in an urn of the family's selection. Loved ones then decide upon the final disposition of the ashes—burial, scattering or even retaining them for the next family death or perhaps for a dual scattering.

I have scattered ashes on behalf of family members many times, sometimes with unanticipated snafus. An avid fisherman passed away recently, and his children wanted his ashes scattered in the nearby river where he had spent many a pleasant evening. When I handed over the urn, the family asked if I would be willing to accompany them and actually pour the contents into the water. I agreed. But on the river bank in December, perhaps I should have held the open container just above the water instead of at waist-level. The howling wind blew a large quantity of the ashes right back into our chilled faces.

The deceased man's children received that ominous affront with good-natured laughter. Their dad, they said, would have gotten quite a kick out of the calamity. The incident reminded me of the day that Ted Kennedy and his family attempted to scatter the ashes of John F. Kennedy, Jr. and his wife Carolyn off the end of a naval vessel in the open sea. With high winds and cameras rolling, it appeared that the ashes blew right back toward the ship.

An active elderly lady of substantial means contracted with me for the direct cremation of her late husband of 48 years. The day I presented her with her beloved spouse's ashes, she asked if I would call the office of their favorite golf course to request a scattering into one of the sand traps. This sweet couple had played there in a mixed golf league every Thursday for several years. She even specified the sand trap on hole number six, since her husband had been stuck there on several occasions.

I had experienced such a request before, and in each case had been denied—so I informed her of that fact, and then offered a sneaky alternative. Why not go out to the course as usual on Thursday with her husband's ashes quietly stashed in her golf bag? Upon reaching the designated trap, she could open the container, pour the ashes into the white sand and then use the provided rake to mix them. She called me on Friday morning to report that the deed was done, even though she felt like a criminal the whole time.

Direct cremation is another area where the consumer can save hundreds of dollars merely by price shopping either by phone or in person. In my area direct cremation charges range from a low (at my own funeral home) of $895, including the crematory fee, to a high of $2495, not including the crematory fee. Crematory operators charge from $180-$350 to actually cremate the body, and I include that fee as part of my service charge, although most funeral homes do not. Among other states, Florida and California are popular cremation states and are known for conducting price wars for services. Billboard and telephone book advertisements tout the best prices offered by funeral homes and even direct-disposal operators. It is not uncommon to see a billboard in California offering immediate cremation for $395.

Cremation with a memorial is the second category. Basically the same service is offered as in direct cremation, but with an actual funeral ceremony conducted without the body present. Obvious extra charges would be incurred for use of the funeral home or church chapel, an obituary, a register book, clergy and perhaps flowers. Funeral directors are much happier when a family decides to have a memorial service as opposed to mere direct cremation, as a little more money can be made, and an obituary can appear in the newspaper, which is great advertising. Charges for cremation with a memorial service, like any funeral home service offerings, vary tremendously, so again, the consumer is encouraged to shop around.

A complete funeral service followed by cremation is the third category and a growing phenomenon within the funeral industry. The body is embalmed, dressed, placed in a rental casket (or even a purchased wood casket), and a visitation and funeral service are conducted traditionally—the same scenario that precedes a ground burial. The obvious difference is in the final disposition of the deceased. Instead of loading the casket into a hearse for a procession to the cemetery, the family and friends leave the funeral home, and the body is then cremated in private. This trend is a result of ever increasing prices charged by cemeteries for grave spaces and opening and closing the grave. Families have told me that they are happy to have a complete traditional funeral ceremony, cremate the deceased loved one and not pay $2,000-$3,000 to a cemetery for ground burial.

Cemeteries are also feeling the effects of the cremation trend and fewer ground burials. To offset the decrease in cash flow, operators have for years sold burial vaults, monuments and markers, and now even caskets. In the early 1970s, funeral directors and cemetery operators began what is now an ongoing adversarial relationship. Directors took offense at cemetery operators engaging in the sale of and profiting from items that were once their exclusive domain.

When cemeteries first began to sell burial vaults, funeral homes dismissed it as a passing fad. Soon consumers would realize the error of their ways and stop buying products from vendors who had no business selling them. One early problem with cemetery vault sales was that cemetery personnel did not know the difference between a concrete box and an actual sealing vault. And since consumers had even less knowledge, many times a cheaply made fragile box was placed in a grave with the assumption that it was a sealed vault. Funeral directors banded together at one point to try and stop cemetery operators from selling what was thought of as traditional funeral merchandise without a director's license. That attempt went nowhere, and cemetery operators still actively promote burial vaults.

The fact that the cemetery usually stores the complete burial vault outdoors until needed is another thorn in my side. Concrete burial vaults stored in the heat, the cold, the rain and the snow lose significant strength over time and become very fragile indeed. I have seen several occurrences of cracked cemetery-provided burial vaults being installed in graves, even though structural integrity was clearly lacking.

A cemetery where there are either very few or no upright monuments at all is referred to as a memorial park. Memorial gardens, burial park—names given, I suppose, to take away some of the sting associated with burying the dead. Forest Lawn Memorial Parks, with several locations in the Los Angeles area, takes pride in the fact that there are no upright monuments to clutter the park-like setting, and the beautiful rolling hills attest to that. Flat bronze, ground-level grave markers are barely visible from a distance. You have to literally walk right up to a selected grave site to find out who is buried there. Forest Lawn was probably the initiator of the combo concept of a burial park with a funeral home within the same location. It makes sense to have "everything in one place," to quote a 1940s Forest Lawn newspaper ad. Everything includes cemetery property, crematory, mortuary, even flowers and grave markers available for purchase.

Forest Lawn's founder met tremendous resistance from area funeral homes when the concept was first introduced. However, Forest Lawn prevailed and is the largest such combo operation in the United States today, still owned and operated by the same family. It's another idea whose time has not yet arrived in my neck of the woods, where the funeral industry evolves at a snail's pace.

Tissue banks from around the country are becoming more aggressive in their quests to acquire hearts, lungs, kidneys, skin, eyes, ears, bones and other harvestable human body parts. Many hospitals' death reporting forms even include spaces for families to check whether they wish the eye bank, ear bank or any other tissue retrieval organization to be contacted.

I happen to be a big fan of organ donation. An unbelievable amount of good has come from it, and we all might need a new part or two someday. Young people involved in accidents who are brain dead are ideal candidates. Their bodies are kept alive for transplantation once family members say goodbye and grant their permission. I am quite surprised, however, that even elderly bones are in demand. Apparently they can be crushed into a fine powdery mix and used for knee replacement surgery.

My only problem with tissue donation is the lack of expediency. Educating the public, making funeral directors and families keenly aware of their valuable service is all well and good, but when the time comes to actually remove the needed tissue, it takes too long. I have had to wait more than a day on several occasions before I could retrieve a body to conduct the funeralization. Embalming is more difficult after it has been kept in a hospital cooler for several hours.

Digging up a casket and vault containing dead human remains and removing said items either to another location in the same cemetery or to a different cemetery is known as exhumation. Mysterious murder cases over the years have actually been solved by exhuming victims for second autopsies. I have witnessed several disinterments over the years. This process occurs more frequently than one would imagine.

We funeral directors can observe firsthand whether or not a burial vault did its job, or if a casket has remained intact, or even upon opening one long-buried, whether embalming was performed adequately. I have seen varying degrees of rusted out-caskets where no burial vault was used, along with pristine-looking caskets that have been inside burial vaults for over 35 years. In many disinterment cases, the casket is opened for curiosity's sake, and most times the sight we behold is extremely unpleasant. What is left of the human form after 40 years in the ground is a blackened skeleton. After the flesh deteriorates and drops off, black mold covers everything in sight, including the interior of the casket. I once observed the aforementioned scene with a notable exception—the necktie of the deceased looked brand new! The suit coat, trousers, shirt, socks and shoes were all but disintegrated. Yet the polyester necktie remained in place and was still as neatly knotted as it had been 40 years earlier.

Cemetery mistakes are the chief cause of disinterments. Perhaps an old caretaker kept all records in his head, not on paper, and would often bury someone in the grave of his assumption. Such an error might not be noticed for months—but in many situations the family immediately recognizes that their loved one is about to be placed in the wrong grave. That's one reason that cemeteries require families to sign for burials before the funerals take place. It limits the cemetery's liability. A significant number of site disputes are probably never settled correctly because families who continue to complain are told that since they were in such a state of grief at the time of signing, a bad memory could be to blame.

I haven't seen a coffin in probably 35 years, so if I encountered one today, it would no doubt be a collector's item. Count Dracula is the last individual I can recall as having reposed in one—wide at the shoulders and narrow at the waist. Since 1927 the receptacle to bury the dead has been called a casket. "Coffin" is the outdated term used by the uninformed ("Wow! That's one fancy coffin!") and mainstream media-types, who through very little research could easily ascertain how improper it is.

I can almost forgive the casket-buying consumer for such uninformed terminology, because he represents legions of Americans who deny death and wish to strike it from all conscious awareness. However, respected anchors who spout commentary from television news desks or columnists who philosophize in weekly newsmagazines should do more homework. I'm fairly certain, after all, that feature story writers in big city newspapers hardly ever rush to their on-the-scene scoops in horseless carriages.

Another clarification of terms is necessary when detailing funeralization events. A visitation, sometimes still referred to as a "wake," which long ago meant staying awake to spend time with the deceased and his family, is still the act of spending time. Also acceptable are "viewing," literally meaning to view the deceased, and "visitation," meaning visiting and paying respects to the dead person and his or her surviving family members.

A funeral service or funeral ceremony is just what it says—a period of ritualistic actions, usually coordinated by a leader, to pay homage to one who has died, with the body of that honored person present. A memorial service, or simply, "memorial," is much the same as a funeral service, only the body is not on site. A memorial service is commonly conducted after someone has been cremated, and there is obviously no body to view.

Perhaps my thoughts on this subject are much ado about nothing, but I feel that the services I perform daily should be described with the utmost correctness, if for no other reason than respect. Funeral and burial rites can only be conducted one time for each person. If something is attended to improperly, we can't exactly ask for a do-over.

I have noticed that newspaper writers enjoy taking poetic license by referring to a casket in one paragraph and then calling it a coffin in the next. Also, obituary writers in most major newspapers are merely entering detailed information dictated by funeral homes. Since there is a lineage charge, one can submit whatever data the family desires with no editing.

But it's when an obituary is composed by a feature writer for a celebrity or high-profile death that problems begin. Rarely do those obituaries end properly. They include such errors as "Funeral services" will be held or "Memorial services" will take place at such-and-such a day and time. Well, there is only going to be one funeral or memorial service. In a Catholic obituary we never state, "Masses of Christian Burial will be held...." In a Jewish obituary we never say, "Shivas to be observed at...."

Funeral directors themselves can sometimes be blamed for poor obituary writing; most are in fact compiled and written by the director making the arrangements. One common blunder is referring to certain relatives as "brother-in-laws," as opposed to "brothers-in-law."

My personal pet peeve, however, is obits which list the order of events in reverse, with the funeral service mentioned first and only then the visitation or calling hours. Chronological order is far easier for readers to follow. Newspaper writers also commit errors that to me are unforgivable, such as spelling "cemetery" with an *a* or by intending "interment" for burial, but calling it "inturnment"—which is what happened to Japanese Americans during World War II.

Even well-meaning family members who try to assist in the compilation of obituary information are guilty of embarrassing snafus. A few people intentionally omit naming certain irritant brothers, sisters or cousins. But others unwittingly hurt the feelings of grandchildren or siblings by referring to only one as "Mom's favorite grandchild, Freddy," or by saying, "survived by three sons, especially her special caregiver, Tom."

During every stage of the funeralization process so much pain can be avoided. All you need is the trusted guidance of a director who displays professionalism and integrity, is willing to take the time to find out what you really want, need, can afford and feel is appropriate—and also is happy to help with the obituary's proper wording.

NINE

"As Soon As We Sell Dad's House, We'll Pay Your Bill."

*Who price-shops and who doesn't, who pays
on time and who doesn't, and why today's
funeral directors rarely extend credit*

I once worked for an employer who simply could not understand it if a family opted for limited offerings or purchased inexpensive merchandise. "We can't stay in business if we keep selling those tin cans," he'd remark, referring to our low-end caskets. He became especially irate if a family chose immediate cremation—so much cheaper than ground burial—and would be absolutely incensed on the rare occasion of body donation, since our funeral home was merely required to complete a few forms and then transport the deceased to the medical school.

A man in the price-shopping mode called one morning and inquired about the cost of our service for exactly that. His mother had died, and she had a prearranged agreement, but the son still needed to go through a funeral home to finalize her plans. When I told him that we charged $350 for body donation, he questioned the validity of our pricing and commented that our service in this case was nothing more than a glorified ambulance run. He then wished to speak to the owner. I handed the phone over to my employer—who immediately hit the speaker phone button, instructing me to "listen and learn."

His initial tone was pleasant as he explained to the caller that our price included the cost of having two men remove his mother's body from the hospital, the use of the vehicle for transportation and the secretarial expense needed to complete the necessary documentation. The caller then went into a bargaining mode and asked if we would perform the job for $200. Now steaming, my employer uttered the catch-phrase that would become legendary among all of us for years to come: "Sir, why don't you just shove a ham bone up your mom's ass and let the dogs drag her away?" I was shocked, to say the least, especially by the abrupt personality change. The caller hung up in a huff, and my employer smiled and declared, "I hate price-shoppers."

From that day forward, if any family ever mentioned that they were short on funds or that they were looking for our least expensive services, we would all grin at each other (privately) and say, "I suppose we should offer them the ham bone option."

A few of my colleagues still take it personally when a client purchases an inexpensive casket. They see it as a blow to their professionalism. Some are even ashamed to pull a cheaper model out of the hearse, because cemetery personnel recognize quality, even at a distance. That's one reason why so many homes position cheaper caskets away from the display area's entrance, hoping that consumers won't even notice them.

I can relate to both views—up to a point. Families will say, for example, "Dad was a simple man; he told us years ago not to waste good money on a casket," or "Mom would come back and haunt us if we spent a lot of money on her funeral." Legitimate declarations in most cases; however, I have occasionally been informed later by siblings that their mother or father never said such a thing; this brother or sister just wanted more of the parent's estate.

I have also been in situations where survivors expressed horror at casket prices, demanded to see the least expensive ones, and then turned around and purchased a pricier one than intended because they liked its looks. Or they called back the next day to choose a costlier option because they feared that other family members might be upset.

Another former employer was arranging the funeral of a prominent physician and became enraged when the late doctor's wife requested the simplest casket in stock. He angrily informed the woman that in consideration that such a high-profile funeral would inevitably draw a huge, well-heeled crowd, he could not allow her to embarrass him or herself by laying the good doctor to rest in a "cheapo." The widow relented and selected a higher-priced model—but also informed her children that they should call a different funeral home when her time came.

Several years ago a smarmy coworker prided himself on being a casket salesman extraordinaire. He could sell the most expensive units by using some of the oldest, most despicable tricks in the book. He'd drape his arm around a widow's shoulders, stop in front of the costliest casket and inquire, "Wouldn't Ed look nice in this one?" Or, "You know, this is the last thing you can do for Ed." Or, "Think of all the nice things Ed bought for you over the years; it's time you paid him back, wouldn't you agree?" Or, "You can't take it with you. Have you ever seen a U-Haul pulled by a hearse?"

I am still amazed that anyone could possibly garner high-dollar sales from such inane spiels, yet somehow for this guy they worked. He had, however, an affection for the grape, and once was assigned to collect a large unpaid funeral bill resulting from his having badgered a client with little ability to pay. After making several phone calls and getting no response, he returned to the funeral home late one evening to try reaching the debtor at home. He had already consumed a few martinis, and it showed during his conversation. He informed the owing party that if payment was not made in full by the following day, he would go to the cemetery, dig up the casket and vault and store them both in the funeral home's garage until the bill was paid. A bank loan was arranged the very next morning.

Our supervisor was happy with the results, but aghast at the collection method. (Luckily, an emotional distress lawsuit was not initiated.) This same coworker also based his treatment and level of service to a client family upon the amount spent. If an expensive casket was purchased, he would insist that we be extra nice. For a lesser casket, he would ignore them as much as possible. As I said, smarmy. I was definitely learning how not to behave.

Several times each year, a family will demand the finest casket available—and the reasons run the gamut. Wealthy clients, if they don't opt for cremation, insist on the best because that's what the deceased sought in life. Other well-off families are intent on impressing their well-heeled friends and colleagues. They make such remarks as, "Dad always drove a Mercedes-Benz, so we want the Mercedes-Benz of caskets."

Some families assume that the most expensive casket is invariably the highest quality; therefore, the purchase is easily justified. A few will look at every casket on display, and after not finding one costly enough, ask to see a catalog of lithographs picturing the most elaborate solid bronze or solid mahogany options. (Every funeral home has such a book on the premises.)

A staunch Republican friend recently prearranged his own service and selected the exact same solid mahogany casket provided for his hero, Ronald Reagan. Another gentleman had just lost his wife to cancer—who before she died had attended the funeral of her neighbor and was impressed with that neighbor's casket. The husband asked me how much it would cost, and then, based upon my answer, requested one that cost twice as much. His wife, he said, always tried to outdo her neighbor in life, whether it was through purchasing a new car, new appliances or new living room furniture.

Another kindly old man recently selected an extremely expensive casket for his late wife, reassuring himself that she would have thought it was the "purtiest" one available. He also insisted that the entire interior be replaced with a quilt design that his wife had loved, even after I informed him that the switch would cost an additional $500.

More than once I have been informed by a beneficiary, "I have a $25,000 life insurance policy, and I want to spend it all, so there is no money left over for anyone to argue about." Grieving parents also tend to overspend on deceased children. Entering a funeral home often scratches the open sores of both guilt and regret. Even a prodigal child hoping to settle some past parental tiff will purchase a fancy casket to ease a burdensome mind.

As a footnote, research tells us that women are savvier shoppers than men. Whether it is at a clothing store or a funeral home, they tend to shop and compare. They'll consider a casket's attributes—exterior hues, interior fabrics and functionality in general. Women frequently lay burial clothes inside the casket to make sure colors do not clash. Mom's periwinkle suit must pick up the navy of the casket's interior, or Dad's camel sport coat must match the tan pillow. Yet it's still a man's world at the funeral home; the majority of male-headed households leave the casket choice to him. So with the most expensive units with the greatest eye appeal strategically placed right inside the door, any man arriving alone to make funeral arrangements will likely select the first fancy casket he sees.

But just as some consumers insist that money is no object, many more have no desire or no means to spend a lot of money on funeral merchandise.

The lay person should understand that we funeral directors, like all salespeople, feel a sense of pride and accomplishment when "hitting a home run"—selling the most expensive casket on the floor. Just as in a real estate office or automobile showroom, the lucky seller is the envy of his peers. But a few of my colleagues have resorted to stretching the truth and even being downright misleading to avoid selling a cheap casket, especially in the case of an obese decedent, where an oversize (and more expensive) casket must be ordered.

I have heard stories of families being told that the obese loved one can only fit into a certain (very pricey) oversize casket, and there is no alternative. I have also conducted many funerals for families who have been berated for their frugality by competing funeral homes. They come to me because I don't engage in such astonishing trash talk as, "I wouldn't bury a dog in that casket," or, "You're not really going to put your mother in that sardine can."

Less underhanded but equally self-serving are cases where funeral directors have woven their own networking webs by mingling at various civic functions, especially anything church-related. Bingo nights at Catholic churches have long been golden opportunities for directors to press the flesh, hand out draft beer and Cokes and always be certain to pause and fawn over the elderly ladies—who are the mouthpieces of their church. They quickly spread the word when they find a funeral director whom they consider "nice."

One longtime director friend who has since died was once considered the area's king of the church supper. He hit as many as possible on any given evening, and upon his departure he would find the minister, thank him for his hospitality and then slip a crisp fifty dollar bill into his palm—a huge sum in the 1940s. Which director do you suppose that minister recommended whenever a death in the church "family" occurred?

My elderly friend scored big in the 1950s with an ingenious promotional item, again targeting churchgoers. A traveling salesman was peddling high-priced grandfather clock kits. He also had 30 large schoolhouse clocks stored in a warehouse, collecting dust, which he wished to dispose of. My friend proposed that if his funeral home's name were painted on the clocks' white faces, he would buy all 30. Soon 30 local churches had new clocks positioned in their sanctuaries so that the clergymen could see them clearly. Instead of glancing at their watches to be sure their sermons ended by noon, they glanced at these clocks—and at the same time etched the funeral home's name in their minds.

Some funeral directors admit to having been terrible businessmen over the years, due to the trusting nature of their enterprise. When a family comes to us in a time of desperation, many of us find it difficult to bring up finances. I personally always hope that the family mentions money first. Even after three decades, I still find it uncomfortable to question a grieving family about how their bill will be paid.

Some groundwork can be established during the first phone call. My standard inquiry is normally sufficient to give me a clear picture. I ask if grave space is set aside for the deceased. If the answer is yes, that usually means a complete funeral with ground burial, rather than cremation. A family already intent on cremation usually informs me at that point.

I then request that they come to the funeral home and bring along clothing for the deceased, a recent photo, any cemetery paperwork, military discharge papers and life insurance policies. If the family has life insurance, that is normally a good sign.

Many insurance companies accept a funeral home-provided assignment form, which allows the home to assign the proceeds to pay funeral expenses, assuming that the beneficiary of said policy is agreeable. However, in many instances I discover that policies have lapsed due to nonpayment of premiums, or else the death benefit has been greatly reduced because loans have been taken out against it. Other policies have been in force for only a matter of months, and there is generally a two-year contestability clause, which means that the company will likely not pay off on a policy less than two years old. I have seen some very sad faces before me when I have had to report that the policy the family was depending on is no good.

One Cincinnati-area funeral home was caught a few years ago accepting the total proceeds of insurance policies, even when the face amount was substantially more than the stated expenses. On the form where "amount needed" is normally entered, this home would write in "total proceeds." The beneficiary was likely asked to sign a blank assignment form, or else he simply did not read what he was signing.

Life insurance is no longer assumed. Employers tend to eliminate it from benefit packages when cutbacks occur. So the consumer without life insurance is forced to work out some sort of payment plan, and that arrangement usually turns out to be a bad deal for us. Some families request monthly payments of $100—which means a $5000 funeral bill won't be paid for over four years! From past experience I can report that such payments are rarely even carried out to completion. An old funeral director friend of mine once said, "The tears dry up when the bill arrives."

That adage still holds true today. If we directors are not paid within 30 days, we will probably not see our money without a fight. Every imaginable tale has been told: "We're waiting for our income tax refund." "As soon as we sell Dad's house, we'll pay your funeral bill." "We need to sell Mom's car first." "My aunt in Indiana is sending the money."

A classic consumer ploy is when a family calls one funeral home to take care of their deceased father, and that bill is never paid. Later the mother dies, and the family calls another funeral home, with no intention of paying that bill either. Then, a few years later, Grandma passes on, and that same family calls upon a third funeral home...and so it goes.

We funeral directors have been forced to rethink our credit policies. In years past, if traditional collection procedures failed, we merely waited until someone else in that family died. Then we would attempt to collect on both funerals—or at least on the first bad debt—or else we hoped that any family still owing from a previous funeral would call a different home.

As late as the 1970s, very few funeral homes asked bereaved families to sign expense contracts. It was rightly assumed that the bill would be paid promptly. If not, there was no recourse except for a collection agency or else attaching a lien on the responsible party's residence, since we couldn't exactly repossess the merchandise. That's why if there is no life insurance, funeral homes now ask for payment in full before services are even rendered.

Many years ago I accompanied my older brother to Cincinnati's county morgue. In the huge cooler room were five deceased individuals lying on carts. I commented to the attendant that he must be having a busy day. "No," he replied. "Those bodies are being held until the families come up with the money for funeral expenses." That used to be a common practice that is now outlawed; you cannot hold a dead body for ransom. I have held bodies in my funeral home cooler until payment arrangements could be established; however, the only times I did so were at the families' requests.

When families reveal to me that they have no money and no insurance, they are not turned away. Many funeral homes, however, particularly conglomerates, do just that—simply send them elsewhere. But I happen to believe that some relative or friend will eventually come through with funds. So I cut to the chase and simply ask how much can be paid on the spot and then offer whatever service and/or economical merchandise will fill their need. Perhaps we eliminate the evening visitation and have a graveside-only service. Maybe cremation is the answer—avoiding cemetery charges can save thousands. Bartering is a final option. (Shades of Atticus Finch.) I once accepted a conversion van and a pickup truck in exchange for my bill.

Today there is little if any assistance from cities or counties to pay funeral costs. Most have an indigent program designed to provide a decent burial for someone who has no immediate family. A grave space, burial vault, opening and closing the grave and a grave marker are provided at no charge, with the cemetery billing the city. Funeral homes are instructed to place the body in a "reasonable" casket and deliver it to the cemetery for a brief graveside service. The city then pays the funeral home $500.

Many low-income families who have been in dire financial straits for years or even generations are quick to inquire as to what governmental assistance is available. Other families, equally poor, somehow scrape together the money to bury their loved ones, without complaining that the city, county or state should ease their burden. But there have been many occasions where families have heard of this program and assume that it is there for anyone who requests it.

I met with a young lady recently who sat down to discuss funeral arrangements for her recently deceased grandfather. As I compiled the necessary information, I discovered that all of her grandfather's children were deceased, he had no siblings, and the five surviving grandchildren were all he had left. This granddaughter further informed me that the man had no life insurance and was not a war veteran. She then inquired, "Before we go any further, can you call the city building and make sure Grandpa is eligible for a city burial?"

I asked her how she knew about such a thing, since most people other than funeral directors do not even know the proper terminology. She explained that when her mother had died a few years earlier, the family had utilized the indigent burial program, and they had done so again when her sister died months later.

I called the city building, and the man in charge asked me to repeat the family's name, which I did. According to policy, he said, he would need to meet personally with the granddaughter to question her about her financial circumstances. The city was changing its attitude regarding city cases; too many families were abusing the system. Large numbers of sons and daughters were expecting the city to bury their parents...free.

After her meeting, the granddaughter told me that she was shocked and embarrassed when she was asked how much she paid for rent and for her monthly car payment. She was ultimately turned down by the city because she and her siblings all worked, most of them owned homes, and all of them were successfully meeting their car loans. Her case was not helped by the fact that her family had taken advantage of the city's generosity on two previous occasions—probably unscrupulously.

Social Security pays a lump sum death benefit of $255. In years past, anyone who paid into or drew Social Security received that amount. The payment was sent to the surviving spouse—or if there was none, to the funeral home providing services. In 1974 the policy changed. The benefit is now payable only if the deceased has a surviving spouse or minor children.

The Veterans Administration used to pay $450 toward the funeral expenses of a deceased veteran who served during war time. Today that payment is made only if the deceased was drawing a VA pension, was injured in action or died in a VA medical facility. Many benefits are still available to veterans—free grave spaces in a national cemetery (many local cemeteries also offer free graves to veterans), government-provided grave markers and United States flags. The VA obviously pays the funeral expenses of those killed in action. I am surprised that even today there are families who assume that the VA is going to pay all funeral expenses for a deceased veteran.

The state of Ohio ceased its welfare burial award program several years ago. The state would pay a funeral home $750 to provide a "decent" burial for those who were Medicaid-eligible or for those drawing Supplemental Security Income (SSI). At my former place of employment long ago, we conducted several welfare funerals each year, and certain families we dealt with took advantage a number of times. There were three names we all grew to recognize. Whenever a death call was received from one of them, we knew the case would be a welfare burial. I once thumbed through the funeral home's archival records and was amazed at the number of welfare funerals, generation after generation, attributed to those three names. However, I had been to their homes for one reason or another, to pick up a body or to deliver flowers, and I couldn't help noticing that there was always cable television and plenty of beer and cigarettes.

I was called to the residence of one of our frequent recipient clans to remove the body of their late matriarch. The house was full of children, grandchildren and great-grandchildren, along with the family pastor. I was asked to sit down and discuss funeral arrangements. On my way into the dining room, I squeezed past a huge projection-screen television. This was in 1987, when the technology involved a large screen attached to a massive cabinet, housing a twenty-inch inverted television and four colored tubes that projected the image onto the enormous screen.

I sat across the table from the sons of the deceased and their pastor. Directly behind him was an old china cabinet fitted with slats of plywood for video cassette storage. I happened to glance at the row of tapes and saw that this family owned the most extensive collection of pornography I had ever seen assembled in one location. One son noticed the focus of my gaze, coolly rose from his chair and quietly closed the doors of the storage cabinet.

Something else that never ceases to amaze me is the numerous flower baskets that arrive at welfare-case funerals. Whether the service is conducted at the funeral home or at the graveside, basket after basket is delivered. One would assume that senders realize the family is in dire financial straits, and offering money to defray expenses would be far more appropriate. But we humans are a strange bunch. We love to see things with our names on them. Even when an obituary suggests contributions to some worthy organization in lieu of flowers, most folks will do both to make certain that something at the funeral heralds the sender's identity.

My former place of employment used to handle 20 to 25 indigent cases each year, prompting my boss to begin cutting some corners. He decided to use heavy cardboard caskets, normally utilized for cremation, which featured decorative swirl designs in gray or blue. Lids were attached by large staples, which also served as crude hinges for opening and closing.

Indigent funerals were almost always conducted at the gravesides, and we normally opened the casket at the cemetery for the family to view the deceased before the service began. On two separate occasions, I was about to open one of our famous indigent specials, only to have a gust of wind blow the lid right out of my hands. I watched in horror as it bounded across the grass and slammed against the monuments, leaving gathered mourners speechless. Cemetery personnel and I quickly formed a posse to chase the wayward lid. Once it was retrieved, I sheepishly replaced it and hoped it would stay secured.

After this happened a second time, I suggested to my boss that perhaps better caskets might be used. He retorted that he was glad both incidents had occurred; perhaps certain affected families would learn something and pony up the money to purchase more reliable products.

Three Mexican cousins were killed in an auto accident a few years ago, and the family wanted the teenagers sent back home for burial. All three had worked for a landscaping company and, like the rest of the clan, they were illegal aliens with no green cards and no Social Security numbers. Ohio death certificates, which had to be translated into Spanish for international shipment of human remains, contained spaces which required those numbers. I am certain that the family member who arranged for the funerals gave me fictitious ones, but I had no proof. A translator helped to explain to them the requirements and costs involved with international shipment, including air fare for all three and fees incurred by the receiving Mexican funeral director.

The cost for each teenager was $7000, which meant a total of $21,000. Since I was concerned about ever seeing this family again, I insisted on immediate payment before any shipment could be made. The following day one boy's parents brought in a Converse All-Star sneaker box full of hundreds, fifties, twenties, tens, fives and even ones to cover the entire cost—obviously the result of multiple contributions.

Long ago, I used to wonder aloud why black families almost exclusively patronized black-owned funeral homes, and why white families patronized white-owned ones. We all (black and white) go to the same hospitals and cemeteries, after all. My question was answered by a fellow mortuary student who happened to be black. His family owned and operated the busiest black funeral home in Northeast Ohio. He explained that black folks were proud of all black-owned businesses, and even black churches, they felt, deserved ethnic loyalty.

Nowadays there is a small increase in the number of black families being serviced by white funeral homes. The first year of my operation, I was called for service by a black family who had gone price-shopping. They told me they'd felt taken for granted by area black funeral homes. It was simply assumed that they wouldn't even look elsewhere.

So when the deceased's obituary appeared in the newspaper the following day, I received an angry phone call from the owner of a prominent black funeral home. He questioned my intentions and accused me of attempting to move in on "his" customers. I responded by asking him how many white families he had recently served. He scoffed and told me that it was none of my business.

Segregation, unfortunately, still exists in regard to funeral homes. Every director has a "blue" or "red" book. This large volume lists every funeral home in the United States and all foreign countries—a handy reference for out-of-state shipping and receiving of bodies. For each state, cities are alphabetically listed, as is each funeral home with its address and telephone number.

But upon perusing a book from the 1950s, I noticed that after the name of each black funeral home was the designation (COL) for colored. In the 1960s that designation was updated to (B) for black. Today's book uses (BLK).

I have had very little negative interaction with the African-American families I have served. Only twice have I encountered any racially based conflicts. In one case a family requested three limousines for the funeral service. When I informed them of the charge per limousine, a feisty older woman piped up: "I'll bet you don't charge white families for extra limousines." When I explained to her that I did in fact charge extra, and that I took offense at such a remark, she backed off.

Another arrangement conference with a large contingent of family members included their angry questioning of whether "a white devil like you" was capable of applying proper cosmetics and styling the hair of their deceased mother. I assured them that I was quite capable, my backup hairdresser was very experienced in styling black women's hair—and that referring to me as "a white devil" was unnecessary and uncalled for.

"Who's the Hooker with the Minister?"

Whiners, bad apples, altruism,
and why dealing with the clergy
can be so high-maintenance

Legitimate complaints received by funeral directors are taken very seriously. Immediate damage control is of utmost importance, since a family who feels slighted or mistreated in any way will surely call upon a competing funeral home for service in the future.

Most complaints, thank goodness, are minor, usually the result of some miscommunication. Obituaries are the most common snags, where some family member has gone unmentioned or a name has been incorrectly spelled. Such incidences can be smoothed over quickly with no lasting negative effects. We funeral directors compile obituary information from people who are grief-stricken and probably stressed out from lack of sleep, so occasional mistakes are bound to occur.

But it's not always that simple. After having conducted funeral services for a deceased friend, I was delighted when my employer handed me a letter from that late friend's spouse. I assumed it would be congratulatory, perhaps lauding me for my fine job of caring for her family's needs. But as I read the letter I slowly became shocked at its contents. This woman was terribly upset over "many" incidents taking place at both the funeral home and the cemetery. I pored over her virtual laundry list of infractions and decided to call and go over each one.

She was angry about late arrivals being allowed entry into the chapel. I explained that letting people in after the funeral had begun was customary. She was angry about the chapel door squeaking every time it was opened. I assured her that I would spray WD-40 on the hinges.

She was angry about two babies crying throughout most of the service. I explained that such disturbances were common at both weddings and funerals, and it wasn't my place to order young mothers to leave.

Her next problem was with the lounge. There were a coffee pot and a soft drink machine, small tables with crayons and coloring books and several ashtrays, because the area doubled as a smoking room. She was upset that a place where small children played might be filled with cigarette smoke.

She was also appalled that a funeral home would charge fifty cents for a can of soda at her husband's visitation and funeral, thereby profiting further at her expense. I happened to agree about the lounge complaints. I have since made it a point not to allow smoking inside my own funeral home, and I do not charge for Starbucks coffee or soft drinks.

Her next problem was with the cemetery and not enough chairs at the graveside. (Typically, cemeteries set up only a dozen.) She also disliked the large pile of dirt sitting next to her husband's grave. (Also customary for this particular cemetery; it's easier to fill the grave after everyone leaves. Some keep a "dirt box" covered with artificial grass for a better presentation; others keep it in the bed of a nearby dump truck.)

After several minutes I realized that no matter what I said, she was not about to be satisfied. I expressed my regret and hung up with a sinking feeling of failure. However, a few weeks later another letter arrived. Expecting an additional litany of dissatisfactions, I opened it to find to my surprise a letter of apology. The woman thanked me for everything I had done and admitted that her previous venting was her way of dispensing anger she carried due to her husband's early death. I had just happened to be the target.

An elderly gentleman passed away many years ago, and his son, a busy Disney Corporation executive and overseer of Disney World in Anaheim, called me from Los Angeles to meet in Ohio the next day to arrange the funeral. He openly admitted to a blatant disregard for my entire industry, considering all of us ghouls and low-lives intent only on taking advantage of other people's misery. I attempted to allay his concerns, making it clear that any decisions we made that day were not carved in stone, and that he was welcome to go back to his hotel and meet with me again after he'd had time to think things over. He did just that, and the next morning we arranged for his father's immediate cremation, with the ashes shipped to California for scattering into the Pacific Ocean near Santa Monica.

When I informed the son that his total charges were under $1500, he was flabbergasted. His uncle had recently died, and the same services in California had cost him over $5000. I responded that obviously the standard of living was much different out there. The man later sent me a nice thank-you note with an additional check for $1000 and a permanent gate pass for my entire family to Disney World.

The funeral industry, like all enterprises, definitely has its share of bad apples. Terrible scenarios abound—from cremating the wrong body, to cremating more than one body at a time or even cremating a human and a pet in the same retort, to clear cases of taking financial advantage of the vulnerable elderly. A close competitor was caught off guard by a local television news team working on an undercover story concerning price gouging. Dubious acts were caught on tape, such as an inadvertent demonstration of how this funeral director intentionally steered consumers toward expensive high-end caskets in his display room.

Some operators write down license plate numbers of cemetery visitors, then call them later to sell grave spaces, burial vaults, caskets or markers. Another ploy is to insist that the entire family of the deceased come to the cemetery and sign a form to verify the grave, even if it has already been owned for many years. Once the family arrives, there's a slick attempt to hawk additional graves, mausoleum crypts, markers, vaults and caskets. In cases of immediate or direct cremation, families are often told that expensive hardwood versions must be purchased—which is not true. High-pressure, commissioned salespeople may be introduced as grief or family-service counselors in an attempt to sanitize their image. In reality, they more resemble used car salesmen, and their pitches border on the unbelievable: "Since we are all going to die, you had better buy from us today." Or, "What if you get hit by a bus on the way home, and you aren't prepared?" All present might also be encouraged to purchase their own graves right on the spot, so that they can "enjoy eternal rest together as a family." If that suggestion is met with resistance, the "counselor" then scolds the family, remarking, "I can't believe that you people would want your loved ones buried next to a bunch of strangers."

A memorial park operation in my area has put on some memorable sales-generating events, offering a free Butterball frozen turkey to anyone who comes by to view the property or restaurant gift cards to those willing to listen to pitches describing the newest sections. (As with any major purchase, do not go to a cemetery sales conference alone.) Since people are always happy to accept freebies, another park ploy that has worked well is to offer a free grave for any veteran whose spouse has paid full price. Of course, full price for the second grave is the price of two graves anyway. The most targeted group is senior citizens, already hit hard by phone solicitations for replacement windows, credit cards and new mortgages—and now, they are also prime prey for cold-calling cemeteries.

The mean-spirited news media love to rake the funeral industry over the coals, and many national headlines are certainly sordid enough to justify scrutiny. The crematory scandal in Georgia is one example. An operator was found to be leaving bodies to rot in sheds instead of cremating them, because the cremation chamber was allegedly inoperable. He kept the scam going by presenting people with containers of dirt, rather than the cremains of loved ones.

Part of the reason reporters relish such scary stories is our industry's checkered past—coupled with the fact that we deal with people at their most helpless. In the classic movie "House of Wax," the proprietor of a wax museum (Vincent Price) has been horribly disfigured in an accident, so his hands are not as capable as they once were. Since he is no longer able to craft his wax figures, he resorts to stealing bodies from cemeteries. But those bodies, he discovers, are more decomposed than he would like, so he turns to murder and later retrieves his victims from the local morgue. The fresh kills are then covered in wax, making for very realistic museum fixtures. Perfect horror fare...because to the average person, it's almost believable.

Body snatching and grave robbing were once the only ways for medical schools to obtain specimens for study and dissection. In Cincinnati in the 1800s, one man was notorious for supplying corpses at a prolific rate. He would take out his wagon nearly every night to frequent not only small cemeteries, but also Spring Grove, the second largest in the United States and the burial spot of many famous Cincinnatians. At $25 per body, he developed quite a business.

Although the authorities were aware of his actions, little was done to stop him until a seven-year-old child was removed from her grave and her corpse was spotted lying in the grave robber's wagon. This act was hideous enough to prompt the state to enact legislation to allow hospitals to solicit family members' permission to acquire their loved ones' dead bodies.

A California medical school was in the news recently for allegedly conducting a scheme to sell human body parts. Hearts, lungs, kidneys and even eyes were removed from donated bodies and supposedly retained in formalin-filled jars for future study. It was discovered, however, that for a fee many parts were being shipped elsewhere, still in their preservative states. Other medical schools and even some very peculiar individuals were buying human organs.

Someone close to the case reportedly said that private purchasers were displaying the parts on bookshelves as macabre conversation pieces. Specific orders were even placed, such as someone from New Jersey requesting a complete pristine human brain. It was to be sealed and shipped in a preservative-filled container. But it was packed improperly, and a tremendous odor was detected in the shipping service's warehouse. With the return address marked clearly on the label and a small amount of detective work, the jig was up.

Since vital organs for transplantation must be removed before death and under sterile conditions, these organ snatchers were clearly profiting by operating a human chop shop—sort of like stripping stolen cars and then selling off the parts. Some local coroners' offices have been admonished for removing the corneas of decedents without the relatives' permission. And here in Cincinnati a photographer was charged with abuse when he visited a morgue to shoot pictures of corpses holding such objects as keys and musical sheets—and then calling it "art." Family members were repulsed—and very, very angry.

In the early 1980s I was a member of a committee which coordinated the disposition of mass casualties following natural and human-error disasters. In the three years I served, no such disaster occurred, so my training was never utilized. But we were shown videos from two separate airline crashes that shocked me—not because of the utter destruction, but because of the actions of the first responders.

Some were firefighters and police officers; others were merely gawkers who happened upon the scene and were then put to work. They were spotted, plain as day, plucking watches and rings from severed arms and emptying cash from wallets. After the money was jammed into pockets, wallets were tossed back on the ground to be discovered later for identification purposes.

A more detailed response is no doubt in force today, as such a disaster would be deemed a crime scene and therefore more vigorously secured. Still, I have witnessed many thefts at accident sites over the years, ranging from a police officer snatching a pack of cigarettes from a victim's shirt pocket to actually removing money. The police obviously pull a wallet from a man's pants pocket to establish identity through a driver's license, so I suppose that makes it incredibly easy to make a "withdrawal." Bereaved families have complained to me that they know money was stolen, but they lack any way to prove it. That's why I always make sure that a minister or family member is in the chapel with me at a funeral's conclusion, so that when the casket is closed, anything that is to stay with the deceased stays there—keepsakes, photographs or money. If any item is to be handed back to a family member, it is done so immediately and in the presence of a witness.

When making funeral arrangements, the topic of jewelry is always discussed in detail beforehand to ensure that all desires are carried out. When meeting with the elderly, I have noticed that their age group emphatically insists that all jewelry worn by the deceased must be returned. Upon further questioning, it becomes apparent that these folks assume that the funeral director is planning to abscond with any valuables. Such atrocities must have occurred frequently years ago, because that concern seems to be paramount in their minds.

I personally find it hard to fathom, but only a generation ago funeral directors were indeed notorious for stealing. One director friend told me that a coworker back in the 1950s earned a substantial living on the side by removing gold fillings and inlaid crowns (the real McCoy back then, not the plated material used today) from the teeth of decedents awaiting burial. He even claimed that he was given permission to do so by their families!

I once delivered a casketed body to a funeral home in Northern Ohio, and upon my arrival, the elderly owner offered to give me a tour of his facility. As we casually trod through this grand old mansion, he pointed out the impressive curved staircase, the stained glass windows and the thick carpet that had been delivered by a London manufacturer in 1949. The tour's end found us in a dark, dingy basement which housed the preparation room and a cubicle that contained shelf after shelf of unclaimed boxes of cremated remains. On the opposite wall of shelving were several plastic bins full of bloody clothing. On each bin was a typewritten sheet giving a full graphic description of the contents and how they came to be soiled. Why someone would keep bins full of biohazardous material on their premises was beyond me, yet this gentleman seemed proud to show off his collection. He then pointed to a large box full of old hearing aids and another full of chrome-plated heart pacemakers. He told me he planned to sell the medical devices back to the manufacturers someday and net a tidy profit. I left shortly thereafter, thinking that this guy definitely needed to seek qualified psychiatric help.

There are, however, many feel-good stories in our industry, both local and national, that do not receive any attention. I worked for a kindhearted man who desired no publicity. Few were aware that every May he would ask the local high school's dean which students could not afford caps, gowns or class rings. Many participated in graduation ceremonies without ever knowing who their generous benefactor was.

After a tragic accident left seven children without their mother and father, this same man instructed the children's aunt to take all seven to a store and purchase new outfits to wear to their parents' funerals, with the bill sent to him. Of course there was no charge for either of the two funerals.

I learned a lot from this employer. Altruistic deeds are now my hallmark. I might not be making as much money as some of my colleagues, but I'll bet I sleep far better.

In October, 2004, I noticed a small newspaper article concerning the death of a recently identified 35-year-old female. A minister was making a plea for assistance with burial expenses. The woman happened to be a known prostitute, and her death was the result of a brutal beating, rape and being shoved out of a moving car. She had been left on the side of the road with no identification.

On a scrap in her pants pocket was a telephone number. The police dialed it and reached a childhood friend with whom she had once lived as a teenager. It turned out that she's been booted out of her home by an alcoholic mother at age 14 and was on the streets by age 17. Since then her childhood friend had lost all contact with her.

The minister called several area funeral homes to ask if anyone could donate a casket or a bouquet of flowers. Amazingly, he received nothing.

I listened to his incredible tale; then my daughter and I removed the young lady's body from the coroner's office, performed the embalming and set out to see what contributions I could gather myself. I was finally able to obtain a discounted casket and vault, along with a grave space. Township trustees who operated the cemetery agreed to open and close the grave without charge.

The minister reported these good deeds to local television stations, and I was soon deluged with live interview requests. The news reporters seemed shocked that I would perform such a service at my own expense. I was happy for the free promotion, yet also saddened to think that many other directors had the opportunity to offer assistance but did not.

As I've said, I make it a point never to turn a family away because of a dire financial situation. Certain services can be reduced, and less costly merchandise can be substituted in order to make the death care experience affordable. I'm sure there are many other funeral directors out there—I hope so, anyway—who assess no charges for infants and offer free services for police officers, firefighters and military personnel killed in the line of duty. That's typical of most independent family-owned and operated funeral homes, where the hometown director can become a true friend. Conglomerates are far less likely to reduce prices, and outright donations are rare. They also do not wait for insurance payoffs. The corporate "brain trust" wants to be paid immediately; they think the families should be the ones to keep checking their mailboxes.

A truck driver hauling two huge steel coils pulled off the interstate onto the shoulder, perhaps to stop and adjust his cables. Tragically, one coil rolled off the trailer and crushed him. When I arrived on the scene, a wrecker was in the process of raising that coil, precariously suspended by what I thought to be a very fragile cable. I hurriedly assisted in pulling out the unfortunate driver, wanting to spend as little time in harm's way as possible.

I retrieved my mortuary cot and slid it next to the body, which had been smashed from the steel's weight. It resembled what might happen when you stomped on a fat caterpillar. This poor man had been struck by the steel from his groin area up to his head. His internal organs had blasted out from a tear in his side and lay all around him. It was a surreal scene indeed. One life squad attendant stared and pointed: "Look, Bob, there's his heart." It was, in fact, upon further inspection, a lung.

I transported the body back to the funeral home. As I walked in the door, the telephone was ringing. The Ohio State Patrol asked me to check the driver's pockets; he'd supposedly been carrying over $40,000 of the trucking company's money. A patrol officer had searched the truck, found nothing and was resigned to the fact that the money would probably be discovered someday by some homeless guy searching the nearby field for used pop bottles.

I readied a large plastic garbage bag next to the preparation room table in order to dispose of what was left of the driver's tattered, bloody clothing. After peeling away some of his tissue-covered shirt, I happened upon a large wallet with an attached chain, the kind that motorcycle riders carry. I washed off the blood and gore, dried it, and to my surprise found it stuffed full of crisp $100 bills. Briefly, I thought, how handy to have an extra $40,000. But I knew the good Lord would not be pleased, so I called the State Patrol to report my find.

Shortly thereafter, the trucking company's owner phoned and said he would be at the funeral home the following morning. Upon his arrival, he thanked me for being so honest and handed me a check for $1000. My name and picture, labeled "Good Guy of the Month," appeared at many Ohio truck stops for the rest of the year.

Another time I was summoned to a stately old farmhouse to remove the farmer's body—discovered in the concrete block workshop behind his home, where he'd apparently collapsed while repairing a vehicle. Two sheriff's cruisers were in the driveway when I arrived, but no one else was in sight. The coroner had told me that the old gentleman lived alone, with two grown sons living out of state.

I poked my head through the workshop's door and spotted two deputies counting out cash. One was alternately placing bills in one stack in front of himself and another in front of his partner. They both looked up, sheepish and red-faced. An old safe sat below the workbench, its door wide open—-and crammed full of cash.

One deputy remarked, "Well, I guess now we have to include you in the count."

"No, thanks," I replied, and simply removed the old farmer's body.

Funeral directors and the clergy, through regular, ongoing contact, enjoy a close-knit relationship. They are often good friends, golfing partners, sometimes even drinking buddies.

Priests and ministers can make or break a funeral home's reputation. My first year in the business involved working for a man who lavishly bestowed gifts upon the clergy. When a minister first arrived at the funeral home to conduct a service, my boss would hand him a Cross pen and pencil set. The next time the pastor would receive Cincinnati Reds tickets; other times a crisp $100 bill would be pressed into his hand. "These people help us to stay in business," he would tell me. "Go out of your way to treat them well."

For Christmas he would order $100 fruit baskets from a local florist, and we would deliver them personally to area ministers' homes. After about three years, my boss decided to curtail the practice, and you would not believe the fallout. Not only ministers, but their wives began calling us around December 20th, wondering when their fruit would be delivered. When informed that gifting had been cut back, we were termed a bunch of cheapskates. The practice was reinstituted the following Christmas.

A few ministers can be real thorns in our sides. The senior pastor of one large Baptist congregation was not fond of my former boss. The good reverend of 60 years' residence was married to a parishioner 30 years his junior—a woman notorious for her fine jewelry and tight-fitting clothing, much to the embarrassed chagrin of their congregation. The first time my former employer caught sight of the couple was when the reverend came to the funeral home to attend a visitation. My boss asked in a loud voice, "Who's the hooker with the minister?"

Over the next few months of obituary reading, we couldn't help noticing that deceased members of that congregation were being serviced by other funeral homes. When I was finally able to arrange a funeral with this minister, I asked on our way to the cemetery why he was avoiding us. He proceeded to rail on and on about my boss and finally admitted that he'd encouraged his congregation never to enter that establishment again.

Years ago, Catholic parishes were small neighborhoods of only a few streets, and the local funeral home was patronized exclusively by parish members. These days, with folks moving to suburbs and declining enrollments, the relationship has also slowed. Also, Catholic dioceses in some cities have begun building funeral homes on Catholic cemetery property and then goading parishioners into using those homes: "The local diocese would appreciate it if you would consider the funeral home on our cemetery grounds when the need arises." The church's using its tax-exempt status to construct a for-profit funeral home will probably be the last straw in straining our relations.

Since I am often asked, I must say that priest molestation scandals have not surprised me in the least. I heard of such occurrences even as an elementary school student in the 1960s; however, in those days, people kept quiet about them. As a Protestant, I attended the city's public schools, but many of my childhood friends attended the local parochial schools and shared with me some of their encounters.

I also remember my father once questioning a neighbor about whether she was comfortable with her two young sons and their youth group camping out with the parish priest. The woman curtly replied that a priest was as close to God as one could get. Her sons could be in no better place with no better company.

Even after a few incidents surfaced, many parents seemed oblivious to the inherent wrongdoing. Whatever the priests' actions, they must be all right, since they represented the beloved church. One popular priest presided over one of the largest Catholic churches in my area. I had conducted many funerals there over the years. After lunch at a local restaurant, I approached the counter to pay my check, and there sat the priest, with four preteen boys seated at his table. I picked up his lunch bill and waved as I walked away. He motioned me back to thank me and then made an eerily prophetic remark: "Bob, you're paying this check for me because you want my body—just like all of these fellows here. They want my body too."

I left, shaking my head at the crass joke. Only weeks later this priest was arrested on several counts of child molestation. I hope that none of his victims was among those present that day. But I probably know better.

Catholics must be a hardy band indeed to endure scandalous behavior against their children and then watch church leaders using their decades' worth of hard-earned offerings to pay off lawsuits. My childhood neighbors were far from wealthy. I often wondered why their parents struggled financially to pay for parochial school tuition, as opposed to attending free public schools. Since children usually tell the truth (at least until they learn to lie better), I received some unexpected answers to that question.

The youngest child and only daughter of a large Catholic family across the street informed me that her father did not want his kids going to school with black children. Another Catholic friend said that his mother wanted him to avoid classes with hillbillies. Yet another stated that since his mother and father went to a Catholic school, he should too. The most common reason was athletics, a better chance to make the teams. Only rarely did I hear the answer I'd expected: "For the superior education and religious training."

Scurrilous episodes within the clergy are obviously not limited to Catholic priests. A once-respected Pentecostal preacher, a vehement protester against pornography, was cited for having kiddie porn on his office computer. His longtime secretary had been searching for a file, stumbled over the smut and for fear of being implicated herself, she called the police. This minister had been a powerful, impressive speaker who delivered thought-provoking yet comforting funeral messages. I was shocked to hear about his extracurricular activities.

One of the nicest, most respectful ministers I have ever encountered stood before his congregation one Sunday and revealed that he was in the midst of an affair with a parishioner who had sought his help for marriage counseling. He was resigning and leaving his wife and children for her. In another case, I had not seen a certain Methodist minister for many months. After a death in his congregation, an interim minister conducted the service. I asked the whereabouts of the senior pastor and was informed that he had forged signatures on the deed to the manse (his church-provided residence), sold the property and pocketed the proceeds.

A famous media-type once stated that organized religions—specifically, new mega-churches led by handsome, smooth-talking, $1000 suit-wearing ministers—were for poor, ignorant, unedu-cated people with nothing to look forward to in life. I disagree; however, I also question whether the good Lord would approve of the way His Word is being delivered in some arenas.

Many years ago, I held several funerals at a Fundamentalist church, where the minister promoted himself and his facility at every opportunity. "If Mr. Jones could rise up out of that casket and talk to you right now," he'd bellow, "he would tell you to come here every Sunday morning, every Sunday evening, every Wednesday evening and every Saturday evening. If you want to hear the true word of God, then you must come here!"

At one particularly rousing service, he came down from the pulpit and brought the whole front row of family members to tears—of anger. The deceased was a 45-year-old father who'd left a wife and twin 16-year-old daughters. Both girls were high school cheerleaders. The minister pointed his finger directly at them and shouted, "If your daddy could rise from death today, he would tell you two to stop displaying your bodies in wicked ways with those little cheerleader outfits." Although most of the congregation voiced agreement with hearty rejoinders of "Amen, brother," the family was not pleased.

This same minister was known to, in his own words, "tell it like it is." He once declared to those assembled at a funeral service that the deceased, a divorced man and known drinker, was no doubt "in a devil's hell, in a lake of fire, with not a drop of water to cool his tongue." Once again, attending family members were not happy.

This minister's congregation was not shy about sharing their beliefs, either. As I was manning the front door at a visitation one evening, a follower asked me where I went to church. When I responded, she said, "Well, I really feel sorry for you, because you are surely going to hell." When I asked why, she responded that only her church members would ever get to heaven.

I can't understand why religion so often serves to divide people. It reminds me of the joke about two men sitting at a baseball game. The first man states that he is going to move to Missouri, because there are fewer Catholics there, and he despises Catholics. The second man states that he might just go to Texas, because there are even fewer Catholics in Texas. Then a little nun seated behind both men interjects, "Why don't both of you go to hell? There aren't any Catholics there at all."

"What If You Get Hit by a Bus, and You Aren't Prepared?"

*The increasing trend toward conglomerates, high-pressure sales
techniques, how the Federal Trade Commission got involved,
and why you may soon see caskets on display at Wal-Mart*

I realized years ago that the death care industry needed to change.
But unlike electronics and automobiles, where explosive updates
tend to take place regularly, the funeral business moves with gla-
cier-like slowness, if at all. Although more funeral homes are now
modern one-floor facilities, the majority are still converted two or
three-story residences with business taking place downstairs and
the owner and his family living in apartments above. Baby boom-
ers in particular have grown tired of those older homes with too
many steps leading to the entrances, threadbare "movie theater"
carpeting, tiny chapel areas, minimal parking and staffs not open
to anything but solemn, predictable services. I have worked at
places with no handicap accessibility and with lots so small that

visitors were forced to return later when the crowd had diminished or else risk parking in a dark alley. When we actually receive calls in advance to inquire about such things, their importance cannot be overstated.

One major change, however, is the corporate buyout. The funeral industry was ripe for such takeovers. Undertakers once handed their businesses to their sons or daughters, or else transferred ownerships through bank loans to trusted employees. Those days are gone. Owners and their families now realize what cash cows they are sitting on. Even grown children who don't wish to follow in Dad's footsteps still want to see him get top dollar for their share of the assets. A suitcase full of cash can be a powerful persuader.

In the late 1960s a Texas funeral home owner decided to buy out his city's other two big-volume homes, become top dog and stop worrying about competition. The plan in its original form was sound: pool the expensive vehicles, retain current employees for continuity's sake and keep the original names of the two newly acquired businesses so the public wouldn't see any change. Sudden acquisitions usually work well in large cities, where people feel no loyalty and couldn't care less who the owners are. Small towns and suburbs are different. People are far more concerned about who is caring for their deceased loved ones. They want to deal with someone they know from church or Rotary Club—perhaps even a former classmate. They want to see the funeral director himself, or at least his kid, when making arrangements. They also want him at the visitation, and they want him to drive Grandma to the cemetery.

But this owner was not happy with just three funeral homes. He soon began acquiring the largest ones in several neighboring cities as well, often overpaying owners to entice them to sell. Enter the carpetbagger concept. "Carpetbagger" is the word we funeral directors use to describe opportunists who have infiltrated our territory. It has a historical relevance; during post-Civil War Reconstruction, Northerners intent on personal gain headed south, carrying their belongings in carpet-covered satchels.

How can you tell when your area has been invaded by carpetbaggers? First, a marketing staff at the conglomerate's faraway home office bombards the affected community with direct mail pieces aimed at homeowners in the age-45-and-up demographic. Letters begin something like this: "We need your help! Please take a few moments of your time to assist us in determining what is important to you, the consumer, by answering the following questions: Do you currently own cemetery property? If so, where? How much do your funerals cost? Do you prefer cremation? Do you currently have life insurance?" At the bottom of the form is a perforated card for the addressee to return postage free. The direct mail piece is also emblazoned with the recently purchased funeral home's address so that consumers may assume it comes from a familiar business in town.

Responses are followed by phone calls to set up appointments with the corporate funeral home's eager staff of "grief counselors" to sell prepaid insurance policies. Whether responses are returned or not, all targeted consumers are cold-called by hard-sell telephone solicitors (usually at dinnertime), thus reducing the funeral home's credibility to that of telemarketers hawking replacement windows.

Conglomerates have also trolled for potential customers by calling everyone who attends a visitation and has therefore signed the register book. I met a woman who was responsible for deciphering sloppy handwriting, looking up names in the telephone directory and then calling them to say, "Since you were just at a visitation at our Big Corporation Funeral Home, I'm sure you enjoyed our facility and would probably like to have your own funeral here someday. Perhaps one of our fine counselors can set an appointment time to come to your home, so you can prepay your funeral."

When a widow is making arrangements for her recently deceased spouse, the conglomerate "counselor" is also trained to "advise" her: "We will draw up the necessary paperwork to duplicate these services, so you'll have a prepaid funeral plan in place for yourself. That way, when your time comes, no one in your family will need to make any hasty decisions under the duress of grief. Sign right here." Since most folks are in the dark about the funeral industry anyway, this ploy usually works, and the still-sobbing widow probably doesn't even realize what she has agreed to.

After a carpetbagger comes to town, a contract is usually signed with a major casket supplier, such as Batesville or Aurora. A volume discount is then happily offered. Since carpetbaggers purchase far more caskets than family-owned operations, they should rightfully receive that discount. However, the savings are not passed on to consumers. Even the company that I personally feel is a scourge on society, Wal-Mart, through their immense buying power passes on their savings. All corporately owned funeral homes and cemeteries in America should probably be discount houses, since they enjoy a tremendous rebate from the suppliers of their most expensive products—caskets.

With an increase in cremation and a decrease in traditional funeralization, major casket companies are losing market share. Batesville Casket Company has always told funeral directors that we are much like car dealerships. Consumers must come to us, rather than visit a Detroit assembly line, and any authorized dealer will do. So once Batesville ascertains the best distribution and storage plan, you will likely see caskets being marketed and sold through Wal-Mart, Costco or even a stand-alone specialty store.

Conglomerates used to be wiser about carrying out a proper takeover. The former owner would be paid a monthly or yearly fee to stay on, work the front door and otherwise make an appearance when appropriate, so the unsuspecting public would assume that it was business as usual. Perhaps the locals had heard rumblings about the funeral home's having been sold—only to be reassured when seeing the former owner still ensconced in the entryway. In the impersonal metropolis areas, such a takeover usually goes unnoticed. The Frank E. Campbell Funeral Home, undertaker to the stars in the Big Apple, is corporately owned and operated, but Mr. Campbell is nowhere to be seen. Joseph Gawler's, the premier funeral home in Washington, D.C., serving presidents and diplomats, is also corporately owned. Mr. Gawler is not there anymore either.

I have a problem with such name retention. It's misleading. Consolidators are trying to mask new ownerships so that locals will believe that Grandpa is being buried by the same funeral home which buried Grandma. In my state of Ohio, a law once required that after 24 months a new owner must incorporate his or her surname, if only at the beginning or the end. In other words, if Joe Jones purchased the Smith Funeral Home, he had two years to change the name of the business to either Smith and Jones Funeral Home, Jones and Smith Funeral Home or simply Jones Funeral Home. This law was designed to keep owners from taking advantage of some famous person's notoriety. Otherwise you could name your business The Jack Nicklaus Funeral Home. Ohio also didn't allow funeral homes to be titled any other way except by the funeral director/owner's surname. No Chapel of Chimes Funeral Home or The House of Compassion Funeral Home.

Whether it was a payoff by the conglomerates or not, I do not know, but Ohio no longer requires a name change. The original can stay. The business manager must merely have his or her name on a plaque in a visible location.

Just as in most huge takeovers, the bigger it gets, the worse it becomes. A friend works at a home bought for the second time by a conglomerate. He no longer makes any funeral arrangements himself, due to severe criticism by the corporate office. Early on, after having faxed a contract for goods and services for review, he would receive a scathing reprimand. He was told he should have upgraded the client family to a more expensive casket and a costlier vault, and he should have recommended the $300 Thomas Kincade register book package.

On-site decisions, my friend tells me, are no longer permitted. Even a leaky toilet requires a work order forwarded to the California office, where a district manager dispatches a maintenance technician to troubleshoot. Three labor estimates are required, with proper authorization for any repairs costing over $100.

Large conglomerates such as Service Corporation International (SCI), of Houston, Alderwoods of Canada and Stewart Enterprises of Louisiana, to name only three, have encountered some difficulties when buying up funeral home properties in smaller markets across the country. Overpaying means that consumers will experience price increases to make up for it. I have gained quite a bit of new business from disgruntled families who used carpetbagger homes for previous deaths, only to be shocked at the staggering price increases they faced when they returned there for another family member. Some Alderwoods-owned funeral homes actually lowered their prices at some locations after several consumer complaints and business slowdowns.

SCI has also been involved in bad publicity, being accused of unlicensed embalming in Texas and of recycling graves (reselling those already occupied) in Florida. Alderwoods used to be known as the Loewen Group and is now supposedly emerging from bankruptcy proceedings.

Conglomerates are additionally known for hiring newly licensed embalmers and funeral directors for the obvious reason of being able to pay them less. The funeral industry, like teaching, police work or medicine, is a place where there is simply no substitute for experience and knowing the answers to questions before they are asked.

Part of the slowdown in recent high-dollar acquisitions is attributed to the fact that many former funeral home owners are tiring of hearing from past customers about their distaste for the new corporate ownership. Smaller town directors are usually happy when a competitor sells out to a big conglomerate. Since everybody likes to tell a story better than the last person who told it, word travels fast when a home is sold. You can bet that the family personnel will tell anyone who will listen that a carpetbagger is now in operation.

Two decades ago, The Federal Trade Commission began an investigation that eventually led to the 1984 Funeral Rule, which forced funeral homes to disclose their prices and to charge consumers *a la carte*, rather than a blanket service charge. That service charge had included removal of the deceased from the place of death, embalming (if requested), cosmetizing and dressing, arranging/coordination of services, use of facilities for visitation and ceremony, use of related equipment, transportation to the cemetery, secretarial work/bookkeeping, insurance overhead and licensing fees. It was imposed on every client, regardless of need, and presented to each family as a lump sum, ranging (in today's dollars) from $2800 to $4500, depending on the region. The East and West Coasts generally charged at the higher end. The FTC now requires that funeral homes explain to families how they arrive at their amounts, complete with detailed invoices.

Several incidents in Florida sparked the FTC's action. Florida's funeral homes perform many cremations and more ship-outs than probably any other state in the Union. Since retirees from all over America populate the Sunshine State, upon their demise, great numbers are shipped back to their respective hometowns for burial. Tales of families being taken advantage of ran rampant, with reports of full service charges for inexpensive ship-outs to blatantly lying that a casket must be purchased to send a body back home.

Emma Sparkman, an 89-year-old former World War II defense plant worker and a beloved "Rosie the Riveter," accompanied a friend to a funeral home in 1983 to assist in arranging the viewing and ship-out of her friend's recently deceased spouse. The two ladies listened to the funeral director's opening speech and decided to select certain necessary services and a nice solid oak casket. They were not informed that they could simply have had the deceased dressed and placed on a table for a final viewing before the ship-out took place. Instead, they were told that for a viewing of any kind, a casket must be purchased.

On the day of the viewing, Mrs. Sparkman noticed that the casket was obviously not the previously selected pricey solid oak, but some veneered knockoff. On her friend's behalf, Mrs. Sparkman expressed her suspicions to the funeral director, who merely pooh-poohed her concern, assigning it to both ladies being elderly, in grief and perhaps experiencing fading eyesight. Mrs. Sparkman did not buy this explanation. However, her friend saw no need to pursue things further, chalking it up to one of life's unpleasant experiences.

Three years later, Mrs. Sparkman's beloved husband of over 70 years passed away. She shied away from the previous funeral home, calling another in the same city. Her husband Vernon was to be shipped home to Delaware for burial, but a small gathering of Mrs. Sparkman's peers nudged her into holding a brief visitation. After selecting an expensive navy blue stainless steel casket, she asked the funeral director to please leave the showroom so that she might be alone for a few moments. She took a lipstick from her purse, knelt down and wrote her name on the bottom of the casket. At the viewing the next day, although heartbroken and grief-stricken, she thoroughly inspected the casket again.

Sure enough, the same bait-and-switch had occurred. The blue model containing her Vernon was in no way of the same quality as the one shown to her just the day before. The finish was duller, the handles were different, and the interior was not velvet, but a lesser-quality crepe—with no sign of the clandestinely applied lipstick signature underneath. Mrs. Sparkman asked the funeral director to roll the original into the chapel so that the two sat side-by-side. Even with poor eyesight, all assembled could recognize what had taken place, and Mrs. Sparkman was informed there would be no charge for either the casket or the services.

The goods and services shown in this general price list are those we can provide to our customers. You may choose only the items you desire. However, any funeral arrangements you select include a charge for our basic services and overhead. If legal or other requirements mean that you must purchase an item you did not specifically ask for, we will explain the reason in writing on the statement we provide describing the funeral goods and services you selected.

The above statement (or similar words to that effect) is the approved FTC explanation which must appear on any funeral home's general price list. It also comprises what is known as the "non-declinable" charge, an arbitrary amount that homes generally ratchet up several hundred dollars more than necessary. All others are piecemeal—so much for embalming, so much for a hearse, etc. The FTC Funeral Rule, designed to shield consumers from being overcharged, did just the opposite; it allowed funeral homes to attach the non-declinable fee to each arrangement.

Since the FTC mandates that all funeral homes must not only disclose prices but also offer a general price list to anyone who asks for it, since 1984 there has been a huge surge in price-shopping. That spike has increased dramatically in just the last ten years, due to customer dissatisfaction, corporate buyouts, and simply because consumers are smarter yet less loyal and merely want to save money.

Former employers of twenty years ago swore that Armageddon had arrived in the guise of the FTC when they realized that price disclosures must even be given over the phone. Some funeral directors assumed that any price-shopper was a clandestine "plant," sent by a competitor. One former boss would inform callers that they should come by the funeral home in person so that he could show them the list and explain things more thoroughly. If a potential client did arrive, a tug of war of sorts would ensue. My boss would point out certain aspects of the list, all the while keeping his hand on it, hoping the consumer would not try to take it with him.

If families who have experienced recent deaths would allow trusted friends to shop on their behalf, they would probably realize significant savings. A non-grieving friend is better able to compare apples to apples, to declare outright: "Funeral Home A gave us a price of $6500 for casket, service, vault and all out-of-pocket expenses. What is your price for the exact same situation?"

A former employer used to instruct us to offer a $500 discount to anyone who called or stopped by carrying a previous offer. "Even if we don't make any money on this deal," he used to say, "that's fine, as long as so-and-so down the street doesn't get it." I have found that a price-shopper will become a former price-shopper once he feels treated fairly and has received a great perceived value. A happy consumer will nearly always call you back.

I also firmly agree with the philosophy behind price disclosures. Overall, the FTC has helped consumers to avoid being gouged. Offenders have been forced to adjust their prices in order to compete, which makes for a better funeral shopping experience. If your charges are easily justifiable, then you should be happy to share them. I currently advertise prices so consumers immediately know where I stand. I also happily hand out my price list to all who request it, even my colleagues, and I personally go and collect the same lists from them. But I often have to chuckle at the dirty looks I receive.

Arranging for funeral services and merchandise before the need arises is a great concept for all concerned, but a little homework is advised. Inform your immediate family as to your death care wishes as early as possible, even if introducing this topic may be met with disgust. At the very least, decide whether you want ground burial or cremation and communicate that preference clearly. I often meet with bereaved families who have no idea as to the deceased's choice of disposition: "Dad never mentioned it," or, "I don't think Mom would want to be cremated, but she never said one way or another."

I encourage everyone to make a decision and then act on it. If ground burial is desired, select cemetery property and purchase it—and be sure to inform family members. My first experiences with pre-need in the 1970s entailed POD (Payable On Death) accounts set up at a local bank. In one case a retired schoolteacher was widowed and had no children. Upon her death there would be no one to carry out her wishes. So she arranged for her funeral service, selected the appropriate merchandise and paid for everything in advance. That money was placed in a bank account in both hers and the funeral home's name, not to be touched until appropriate proof of death was provided. Yearly interest more than compensated for inflation.

But in the 1970s, banks were paying up to 9% interest, so pre-need accounts only two or three years old accrued far more interest than necessary. That windfall was supposed to be returned to the surviving family or to the deceased's estate, and in most cases that was done. But one former boss used to instruct me to attempt to "upgrade" whenever a large amount of interest had accumulated in a pre-need account.

The 1970s and 1980s were dark periods for abuse in the burgeoning pre-need arena. Funeral industry trade publications were filled with detailed reports of funeral directors pocketing pre-need money. Those funds were deposited into the funeral home's checking account instead of into a separate POD and then were used for day-to-day expenses. Upon the purchaser's death, the funeral home would perform the service and provide the merchandise, with no one the wiser.

Problems occurred when a purchaser decided to cancel the pre-arrangement or wished to transfer the account to another funeral home. The original director struggled to come up with the money, an investigation ensued, and the scam was exposed. Funeral homes received quite a black eye. Insurance-based funding and taking the funeral director out of the mix eventually repaired a lot of the damage. Nowadays, if a consumer has a savings account of $10,000 or a like-value life insurance policy, funding a pre-need through a funeral home is totally unnecessary. Going to a home and prearranging wishes and merchandise and then putting such wishes in writing is an excellent idea in order to save surviving family members from answering tough questions at a time of grief and stress.

Yet many prearrangement clients prefer to pay up front just so they know that everything will be handled properly, that their surviving children will take the least expensive route—and keep the change.

My parting thought on the subject of prearrangements is simple. If you pay in advance, make sure the funds are deposited into an insurance product. Don't let a funeral director or pre-need sales-person talk you into placing funds in the funeral home's savings account. With the onslaught of corporate buyouts, many homes will no longer be privately owned in years to come. Funeral home consolidators are buying out each other's assets constantly—and one of those assets is all current pre-need accounts.

"And So It Begins..."

*Behind the scenes on a death call and
what really happens in the autopsy room*

When the telephone rings in the middle of the night, my semi-awake mind instantly buzzes into action. Since I have a business phone right next to my bed, and I happen to be a very light sleeper, I have no problem answering and sounding as if I have already been awake for hours. I have discovered that even after 30 years in the funeral business I don't mind being jolted from sleep. However, I do admit that it's harder to climb out of those warm blankets during the winter months than the summer, when dawn is not so long in coming.

I sit on the edge of the bed and make a decision. If the death has occurred at a hospital or nursing home, then I will take a shower, get dressed and get moving. If the death has occurred at a private residence, then I will simply wet down my hair, comb it as well as I can, get dressed and really get moving—because a bereaved family is waiting.

The location of the deceased also determines which vehicle I'll utilize. A hospital or nursing home death call can be accomplished with a minivan. A residence requires a hearse. Why? Because many years ago the son of a man who had expired at home was most upset when my assistant and I arrived in a Chevrolet van. As we pulled the mortuary cot out of the back, he exclaimed, horrified: "You came to get my father in a truck?" After that exchange, I resolved never again to attend to a residence call in anything but a hearse.

During the drive from my home to the funeral parlor to retrieve the necessary equipment, I make certain observations concerning this current call. Does the surname of the deceased sound familiar? Perhaps we have served this family before. Did they pay their bill the last time? Do I remember anything else about them? Which cemetery did they use? We already have two other death calls this week; I wonder which day these folks will request for the funeral.

These and many more thoughts bombard me while on the road, with only police officers and drunks out there for company. I arrive at the funeral home, greet my assistant, load up the mortuary cot, and it's off we go. As a teenager, when I assisted my older brother with such duties, he would look over at me as I sat excitedly in the passenger seat of our 1968 Cadillac hearse and remark, "And so it begins..." His reference was to the long, painful odyssey we were about to traverse with a grieving family—beginning with the removal of the deceased and ending with the placement of that dead body in its grave.

These days family members are often present when we make a removal at a nursing facility or even a hospital. In the past, when

I arrived at a nursing home at 3:00 a.m., no one but the nurse on duty was available to help move the deceased out of the bed and onto my cot. Today the family is often waiting—I suppose because nursing home caregivers attend death education classes that stress that family members should be at a terminal patient's bedside for end-of-life support. Most hospitals still require that the deceased be transported by hospital personnel to the facility's morgue, where the body is left in cold storage until the funeral director arrives.

At a residence call there is generally a house full of people gathered at the bedside. This is a scene to be carefully observed and taken in, because important conclusions can be drawn. Genuine sorrow is usually exhibited. However, it is sometimes possible to detect that those sobbing at Grandma's bedside are only upset that their gravy train has been derailed and they can't borrow any more money from her.

More necessary information can be ascertained before the body is even removed. I always ask if the deceased owned grave space anywhere—as opposed to asking for permission to embalm the body. That magic question automatically elicits what I really need to know: Will this be ground burial, mausoleum entombment or cremation? For ground burial it is easy for me to interject, "Then I suppose you'll want us to do the embalming?" For cremation a family usually points out, "And we don't want any embalming."

At the residence we also set a time for an arrangement conference and inform the family of what items they'll need to bring to the funeral home. Since the family is already assembled, they will often tell me which day and time they would like the visitation and funeral to take place. Such information can be noted and save them from having to endure more questions later at the conference.

Our leaving the residence with their deceased loved one in tow can be emotionally wrenching. I have received numerous requests to be sure not to cover the deceased's face. Grown sons may assist us in carrying the cot. Other family members may run down the street after the hearse as we slowly pull away.

Disposition arrangements for a visitation and funeral service or cremation are made; the service takes place, and then we head for the cemetery. All of the links in this chain are arranged either by me or by a member of my immediate family. At some of my previous places of employment, certain key production events were not handled by the same person or persons. One might make the removal; another might arrange for services; another might attend the visitation, and yet another might drive the lead car to the cemetery. When several events are attended to by several different providers with no continuity established, I'm sure the family feels shortchanged and depersonalized. That is why I now see to it that either I or a single family member attends personally to all death care details with any bereaved family.

A death which occurs at a private residence is usually considered unnatural. If someone was injured or extremely ill, why was he at home and not in a hospital? That is the question the police and the coroner are likely to pose upon arrival. With the hospice movement so popular, more and more terminally ill people are choosing to die in their own homes or in those of family members as opposed to the antiseptic settings of hospital rooms.

Hospice nurses and other caregivers are usually present when such a death occurs, or else quickly summoned if needed. A death under hospice care at a private residence is not considered "death without medical attendance." When someone is found deceased at home and not under hospice care, then that case is almost always investigated by the coroner or medical examiner. Some counties in Ohio then require a pronouncement of death by a physician. On many occasions I have had to transport a deceased loved one from his or her place of residence to a hospital, so that one of the doctors on duty can come out to the transport vehicle and pronounce that patient dead. Nine times out of ten, the doctor looks briefly at the deceased, then looks at his wristwatch and says, "Let's call it 2:45 a.m." That is declared the official time of death, even though the patient more than likely expired an hour or so earlier.

Very rarely do doctors come out to a funeral home vehicle completely equipped to make a death pronouncement—no flashlight to shine into the eyes and no stethoscope to detect a heartbeat. I have heard of cases of nursing home patients being transported to funeral homes only to "come to life" during the trip. A colleague once told me that he had an elderly man on his preparation room table and was in the process of removing the man's clothing when he suddenly began to moan and make life-sustaining movements. After a few seconds of being freaked out, my colleague called for an ambulance. The old man was in fact very much alive and was transferred to a hospital where he stayed overnight, and then the next day returned to the nursing home.

I have experienced similar cases where I was just about to roll up the cot to the wrong bed in a nursing home, only to hear that patient still breathing. Obviously I needed to attend the bedside of his or her late roommate. At some older nursing homes, patients are bedded in wards with three or four non-ambulatory people in one large room, each separated by a floor-to-ceiling privacy curtain. Arriving in the dark in the middle of the night, the kindly nurse in charge once commented to me, "Take your pick," as we surveyed a row of four elderly patients, all of whom appeared to be dead.

Before the invention of the stethoscope there were some interesting tests for death. The "fire" test involved holding an open flame to the skin of the potential deceased. If the skin blistered, then the patient was not dead, since skin cannot blister after death. For the "mirror" test, a small hand-held mirror was positioned under the nose or mouth. If the mirror fogged, there was obviously breath. The "water" test was administered by placing a glass of water on the chest, with breathing detected if the water moved in conjunction with the rise and fall.

Even such fail-safe tests were not trustworthy; that is why the term "wake" came to pass. Today it's a visitation period for offering sympathy and support, but originally it meant staying awake with the deceased to make sure he or she was in fact dead. Should a moan, a twitch or any movement take place, then obviously that person was still alive. I imagine such instances occurred quite frequently in the late 1800s and early 1900s, when a comatose patient or even someone who had fainted was often assumed to be deceased.

One coffin manufacturer during the late 1800s devised a notification system to ensure against premature burial. A bell was placed above ground next to the grave with a rope attached and extending into the coffin with one end strategically placed near or in the buried person's hand. Supposedly, premature burials did occasionally take place, as testimonials regarding the efficiency of the bell were lauded in newspaper advertisements. The Sears & Roebuck catalogue even sold it for a time.

The traditional wake, staying up with the deceased, is still sometimes practiced today. In my area there are many families from the Pentecostal southern states, where all night visitations are quite common. Two or three times each year we conduct them, usually at churches. We deliver the deceased by 4:00 p.m., and the visitation continues until the funeral service takes place the following day. It's noted in an obituary as follows: "Visitation after 5:00 p.m. Tuesday at the Church of Holy Grace until the time of the funeral service on Wednesday at 11:00 a.m."

An autopsy may be required for medical or legal reasons—suspected homicide, accident, suicide or other probable unnatural death. Some teaching hospitals request that surviving family members agree to autopsies in order to keep those hospitals' accreditations up to par. As an orderly during my college days, I witnessed hundreds of autopsies. The result was a fervent hope that such a procedure is never performed upon anyone in my family.

A "Y" incision was made by a scalpel on the chest of the decedent. A large knife then pared the muscle and fat tissue away from the flaps to expose the ribs. The ribs were cut away with a cast saw, thus exposing the thoracic and abdominal organs for inspection by the pathologist.

The initial sight of exposed human organs always takes everyone aback. That first glimpse reassures me that there is a God, since all of those organs must work together in perfect synchronization in order to sustain life.

The next sensory experience was the odor. Blood reeks after death, as do stomach contents and obviously the contents of the colon. The vivid colors of human organs stood out as another unique experience—the mottled, black-specked appearance of a lung; the purplish-reddish hue of a heart; the grayish-blue tint and the glistening wet appearance of a kidney; the three-lobed liver, its color matching that of any calves' liver found in a supermarket meat case.

Before proceeding, the pathologist handed me a notepad and pencil, both already stained with blood from his earlier notations regarding height, weight and general appearance of the decedent. I was now the designated stenographer, assigned to note the weight and condition of each organ and also any abnormality detected. I perused the initial notations of the pathologist so that I could be equally descriptive, not wishing to appear inexperienced. Standard initial commentary was already present: "A 54-year-old white female, eyes brown in color, natural hair, streaked in gray. Well-nourished, with all natural teeth present. Surgical scar on abdomen suggests past hysterectomy, with no other scars or anomalies noted."

The pathologist used a large knife to open the pericardial sac, the structure that surrounded the heart. Then with a qualified, deft slice he released the heart from its moorings. The dripping heart was then placed in a stainless steel basket attached to a ceiling-mounted scale so that its weight could be determined. This was critical; if a heart is heavier than normal, that's an obvious red flag and probably the cause of death. An enlarged heart sometimes pinches off the nearby arteries, dramatically decreasing the blood flow. One pathologist used to hold the heart in his hand before placing it in the scale basket, declaring, "Here I have the heart of Alfredo Garcia." It was his idea of gallows humor, perhaps amusing the first time, but quite stale after hearing it for the 50th time.

After being weighed, the heart was then placed on a cutting board, where the pathologist sectioned it, meticulously searching for any abnormality, such as scars from past or recent coronary disease. The remaining organs were removed and examined in the same fashion, with a few exceptions. The stomach was removed, with the contents poured into a stainless steel container for inspection.

The first time I witnessed this procedure I was close to nausea. Stomach acids that had now ceased operation nonetheless carried the familiar odor of vomit. Certain foods do not digest quickly. Salad greens, broccoli and baked potato skins are clearly recognizable among stomach contents, as are drug capsule remains.

I was once instructed to use a screened ladle, much like the device used to clean out a fish bowl, to dip into the stomach of a suspected suicide victim who had potentially ingested many chloral hydrate capsules. It was amazing to observe that such a deed had taken place. I scooped out over 40 capsules, some dissolved, some still very recognizable.

Probably the most unpleasant part of an autopsy is the procedure called "running chitlins." Several feet of intestines curled up in the human abdomen are pulled out a foot or so at a time by an assistant (me) and then handed to the pathologist, who slices open the structures and inspects the interiors for tumors, restrictions or any other abnormalities. Part of my duty was also to squeeze the exterior of the intestine to force fecal material out of the way so the pathologist could obtain a clearer view. That particular procedure took a little getting used to, but after a few times I thought nothing of it.

After having witnessed many autopsies, all of the sights and smells became commonplace. Eventually, as a seasoned veteran, I had to admit I enjoyed seeing young nursing students entering the autopsy theater for the first time. Standing at the head of the autopsy table four across, these fresh-faced kids all wore looks of frightened anticipation. Once the scalpel was utilized, and the body was opened up in all its glory, the countenances changed from nervous grins and smirks to mouth-dropping stares and upper lips curling into mouthings of "Ewww." I often wondered if my experience in the morgue was impressive to these nubile students—or if they felt that the pathologist and I were just a couple of weirdos.

As time went on, and the pathologists, the coroner and I became more comfortable with each other, our back room humor seemed to surface more and more. The coroner at the time rarely laughed, but his dry wit was a hoot. Being an immature 19-year-old who had not yet heard his entire comedic repertoire, I was constantly amazed and amused.

One day we observed the body of a man whose head had been crushed in an industrial accident. The coroner slowly approached the table, peered at the decedent and muttered, "This man will never again find a properly fitting hat." I bit my lip to keep from laughing out loud, but no one else in the room was even grinning. Had the comment been made that many times before?

One male decedent sported the largest penis I had ever seen. I waited in hushed silence to see what words of wisdom the coroner would offer. Sure enough, he winked at me and declared, "No wonder his wife was crying so hard."

On the other hand, a suicide victim sporting a rather smallish member was greeted with the remark, "If I had equipment like that, I would have done the same thing."

All hideously improper remarks, of course, but from then on, decorum was always maintained in the autopsy room, and the coroner was at heart a fine gentleman, whose inventive one-liners continually made me chuckle. He never laughed at his own jokes, though. He also never laughed when I muttered some comment that I believed was vaguely hilarious. He just gave me a blank stare.

THIRTEEN

"Would You Really Let Your Daughter Drive a Lime Green Hearse?"

A reflection on the success and accuracy of HBO's "Six Feet Under"

Claire's mode of transportation was only one aspect of HBO's award-winning series which everyone grilled me about. Would I let my daughter drive a hearse to school? Probably not—but it certainly made a terrific visual. And as a funeral director, I must congratulate the writers and the technical advisor for having presented a largely accurate picture of a family-owned funeral operation, complete with dizzying dynamics and relationship subplots never before explored on television—along with a small, but realistic peek inside a mysterious and fascinating vocation.

As I watched many episodes in the company of fellow directors, in fact, we often exchanged knowing glances. Whether a scene concerned feuding families, people on modest budgets insisting on the most expensive caskets or heartfelt sympathy expressed to the bereaved by Nate and David Fisher, we all agreed: "Been there, done that."

Some of the grittiest details were things that only we would notice. One episode from the fifth season, for example, featured an irate Vanessa storming into the prep room to confront Federico. He was in the process of raising a decedent's leg high in the air with his left hand and holding in his right a set of forceps grasping a white plastic AV plug. Its purpose? To be twisted into the anus and/or vagina of the deceased in order to seal the orifice, thus avoiding any embarrassing leaks or discharges while reposing. Too graphic, you say, even for HBO? Not at all. First, most viewers had no idea what was going on. Second, for those of us in the trade, it provided a riveting touch of authenticity.

Pre-SFU, most movies and television episodes depicting funeral services seemed eager to portray their directors as pale, somber, black-garbed super-salesmen far more intent on separating consumers from their wallets than on consoling them. Perhaps that's one reason our image still suffers at times, why people are shocked to learn that we actually have a sense of humor, and why we still deal constantly with absurd questions regarding whether dead bodies truly sit up, make noises or continue to grow hair and fingernails. "Six Feet Under" helped to make tremendous strides in not only humanizing us, but also in conveying to the public our proper place in society as providing a much-needed service.

Nate's poignant conversation with the elderly gentleman who did not want to leave the funeral home after his wife's visitation had concluded was classic--and very typical. Older couples may have lived together for decades. Now one of them is gone, and the other faces a dreadful emptiness. Nate showed proper compassion toward someone unwilling to return to a silent house; he simply sat down next to the grieving man and let him talk. Any funeral director worth his salt is, above all, a good listener.

There are comical aspects to our business as well. The stripper who was electrocuted when her cat pushed electric rollers into her bathtub tested Federico's breast-positioning skills. Her friends were duly impressed with the lifelike uplift of her assets as she lay in the casket. When questioned, Federico admitted he'd placed a cat food can under each breast. While the idea was intriguing, I'll probably stick to my own tried-and-true method, filling brassieres with just the right amounts of cotton. On occasion I've overdone it, but each time, the surviving husband has expressed approval with a hearty thumbs-up or even a wink through tear-soaked eyes.

The series included only a couple of misleading embellishments: The Fisher & Sons Funeral Home, like many older establishments, was situated in what was once a grand old residence, complete with its outdated basement prep room where embalming and dressing took place. But the Home always seemed to acquire its bodies with amazing speed. In reality, the Los Angeles County Coroner performs such a staggering number of autopsies and examinations that releasing even a single body could take several days to a week. Nate, David or Federico would not likely drop by on the very day of someone's death and return home that evening with the decedent already in tow.

Also, David's fear that Mitzi, representing the scary, deep-pocketed corporation, might buy out the competitor down the street and eventually put the Fishers out of business was probably regional. Perhaps in Southern California there's less personalization and therefore less loyalty. In the East and Midwest, however, funeral directors are often trusted friends who secure much of their continued business through word of mouth. If a family-owned home sells to a faceless, out-of-state consolidator, area consumers hear about it and then become understandably skittish about handing over their beloved family members to total strangers.

I would have enjoyed seeing at least one episode dealing with the inevitable hustle and bustle of a funeral home's busy streak. Several days filled with nonstop, breakneck arrangements, embalmings, dressing of bodies and placing them in caskets, and then hoping everything had been attended to properly and would run smoothly would have been illuminating, to say the least. Oddly, no one ever seemed to be fully present at what eventually became the Fisher & Diaz Home. I can't help wondering who answered the telephone, who greeted walk-ins and who sat down with those wishing to learn more about pre-need contracts.

Years ago, some of my friends expressed horror at the prospect of a TV series dealing with the death-care industry. Four seasons later, those same people couldn't get enough of it. Creatively, you could hardly do better than to begin each episode with a death—followed by a conference with the decedent's family and some sort of off-the-wall request or unique confrontation. Thanks to "Six Feet Under," no individual preference regarding a loved one's send off will ever again seem too bizarre. No flare-up among relatives will ever take anyone by surprise. And best of all, every casket viewing room will forever be known as "Casketeria."

The final episode was surprisingly disturbing to some of my friends and even family members—but I found the scenes depicting how each main character died both touching and reassuring. After all, we can't deny the fact that each of us will someday expire, and we can't possibly know when. Most reassuring of all was that several earlier episodes made clear the possibility that the main characters might not survive Nate's death. For weeks it seemed apparent that Ruth, David, Claire, George and Brenda were all losing their grips on reality.

But just as in the many thousands of cases which I have observed, they peered over that cliff into an emotional abyss—and decided not to jump. Instead, they backed away and reclaimed their inherent strength, along with their own lives. Finally, they united to toast Nate rather than to continue to mourn him.

Life went on. Just as it does, however miraculously, for most of us grieving for those we love and have lost.

"You Sound Just Like Him."

*A funeral director's son speaks out on high standards,
learning patience, being frequently mistaken for "the man"
and how he hopes to continue his father's legacy*

One day when I was around 12, my dad came home boasting of a pocketful of change he'd won at poker. Apparently when there was nothing to do at the funeral home where he was employed, he and his coworkers would while away the afternoon by playing cards. As he described the various hands which had made him that day's "big weener," as he put it, I couldn't help thinking that anyone who played games while on the clock must have one terrific deal. "That," I told myself, "is the job for me."

More seeds were planted each time Dad brought home yet another gruesome tale of unidentifiable remains and then proceeded to tell it at our dinner table. Although he had my rapt attention, my mom wasn't exactly thrilled—-so as I grew older, Dad began taking me outside on the porch whenever he felt the urge to describe one more eyebrow-raising story about his day.

Around the time I decided to attend college to major in mortuary science, my dad was experiencing the itch to stop working for "the man" and become "the man" himself. So in 2001 he opened his own funeral home and was finally able to run things as he saw fit. By then I was completely aware that history would repeat itself. I would, like him, set myself up for years, perhaps decades of working for somebody else—but at least this time it would be my own father. How hard could it be?

What I didn't yet realize, of course, was that Dad would hold me to far higher standards than he would any other employee. Even today, regardless of whether we're embalming, dressing or just cleaning up, if things do not take place in the manner or even the sequence which my father expects, then everything I have done is for naught. I've wasted my time—and far more importantly, his. His voice rises to an "outside" level, even though its only destination is my ears, a mere two feet away.

On a few occasions I've had to admit the yelling was justified. My thought process, which darts from one end of the spectrum to the other in the wink of an eye, might sometimes be described as scattered.

A woman phoned our funeral home one day to inquire where she might send flowers for an upcoming service. I told her she could just send them to the church of her choice—not realizing that the deceased's family wasn't holding a church service, only brief remarks following a visitation. Of course Dad used his "outside" voice to proclaim that it was always my responsibility to find out what was going on without assuming anything.

Another time a young woman had passed due to cancer, and her cemetery procession of devoted friends and loved ones was extremely long, about 75 cars. The first half of the line pulled out of the church's parking lot successfully. But then one car made the mistake of stopping, and oncoming traffic began whizzing by—a serious breach of funeral etiquette, but that's a whole other story. By the time the latter half of the line attempted to get moving, each vehicle had to wait for a traffic lull.

I sprinted down to the highway's nearby intersection and stopped the oncoming cars to keep the rest of the procession together. But once again, I made the mistake of assuming. I thought Dad had made a right turn out of the lot instead of going left. So I sent the second half to the right, and nobody who headed in that direction ever made it to the cemetery.

Several family members called the funeral home over the next half hour, attempting to locate the grave site, and one man in particular returned in person to insist that it was our home's fault for his not being there. He kept saying, "Now, I am not blaming y'all, but I don't know who else's fault it could be."

After hearing that about ten times, I'd had enough. Loudly and harshly, I blurted, "Sir, you <u>are</u> blaming me!" He fired back, "Boy, I'll whoop you right where you stand! Don't you get tough with me!" I snickered, wondering if he was planning to hit me over the head with his AARP membership card.

Needless to say, my dad was not thrilled. Even my mom was upset. And it pains me to confess that both of them were legitimately peeved. Tolerance back then was not my strong suit. I hadn't been seeking a way to resolve the problem so that all of us could walk away happy; instead I'd taken a defensive stance, ready to step outside and engage in fisticuffs if needed. I clearly had a lot to learn.

But gradually, things got better. One day after lunch, a gentleman came in and told me that his father was being cared for by Hospice and had only a few days left. I suggested a prearrangement and filled out biographical information for the impending death certificate. We chatted for another fifteen minutes, and he agreed to call us when the time came.

A few days later when we got the notification, I was out securing a doctor's signature on another death certificate and braving the icy personality of his receptionist. (Medical receptionists generally consider people like me total nuisances.) When I returned to the funeral home, Mom told me that Dad had already left to pick up the body, but the son and his wife were now present and waiting.

I sat down with them, discussed merchandise and services, and before I knew it, all arrangements had been completed. Everything had gone smoothly. The following day, after I'd made my usual rounds, Mom told me the gentleman had just dropped off his father's clothing and paid the bill in full. He'd also told her what a nice person I was and how calm, professional and knowledgeable I'd been. I'd never expected that kind of a compliment so early in my career—particularly since during the entire meeting I'd been telling myself, "Don't screw this up. Give him the correct price, and calculate the sales tax accurately."

What have I learned over the years from my father? That being a renowned and respected funeral director with a sterling reputation for treating other people well requires constant effort and attention to detail. It's about far more than just working visitations, keeping up on paperwork, missing your son's baseball game or leaving a holiday party early. It's also about compassionately helping another family from beginning to end through one of the toughest ordeals which life inevitably hands us.

Dad has also taught me that in most cases, the customer is right. Sometimes, regardless of the business you're in, whatever you do will never be enough. So Dad has repeatedly stressed the virtue of patience and the need not to get worked up over uncontrollable variables. Patience was apparently not a gift that God ever thought Websters should have. I've had to work at it. But I've learned that with patience comes experience, and with experience comes confidence.

So much of this job involves waiting. When things are slow, we wait for the phone to ring. When a death occurs, we wait for a son who lives 25 miles away to come to view his mom before we can carry her away. All of the puzzle pieces must line up and fit together, and some outward force is needed to push them in the right direction. In every case, once I figure out how to harness that force, then apply it appropriately, this business becomes the most rewarding, fulfilling thing I could ever imagine.

I've seen the way people greet my father at a visitation, or anywhere in public for that matter. They're so warm and friendly, so genuinely glad to see him. They really want to hear about his business and about how our family is doing. And we know they'll call us whenever the death of a loved one occurs—because of the kindness and concern that my dad has always projected.

What's comical, though, is how often we are mistaken for each other. Over the phone our voices sound nearly identical. Whenever I answer with a hearty "Webster Funeral Home," the response is almost always, "Bob?"

"No. Michael."

"You sound just like him."

"I know. Please don't hold that against me."

At visitations I often hear, "Ahhh, so you are Bob's boy," or, "Okay, now I can put a face with the voice." Soon I hope it will be, "Hey, good to see you, Michael. You keeping that old man of yours out of trouble?"

Yes. I am. Just as soon as I can find him a hobby.

Printed in the United States
69077LVS00004B/22-120

9 781425 956592